BETTY

The Story of Betty MacDonald, Author of
The Egg and I

Anne Wellman

Copyright © 2016 Anne Wellman

All rights reserved. No part of this book may be used or reproduced in any manner whatsoever without written permission.

First Printing March 2016
ISBN-13: 978-1493662425

Table of Contents

Map of Seattle and the Olympic Peninsula......................2

Introduction..3

Betty and Bob...5

Beginnings..7

Betty and the Chickens...41

Betty and the Great Depression..67

Betty and the Plague...105

Betty and the Island 131

Betty and Fame..159

Betty and the Law 205

Bob Heskett..223

Betty and California...225

Legacy...249

Afterword...259

Bibliography and References..267

Acknowledgments

My thanks to Jill Andrews for kind permission to quote from her mother Blanche Caffiere's book *Much Laughter, A Few Tears*. I am grateful also to Professor Beth Kraig for her assistance in providing access to her work on Betty MacDonald.

Every effort has been made to trace the holders of photography copyright. Any inadvertent omissions of acknowledgment or permission can be rectified in future editions.

Seattle and the Olympic Peninsula

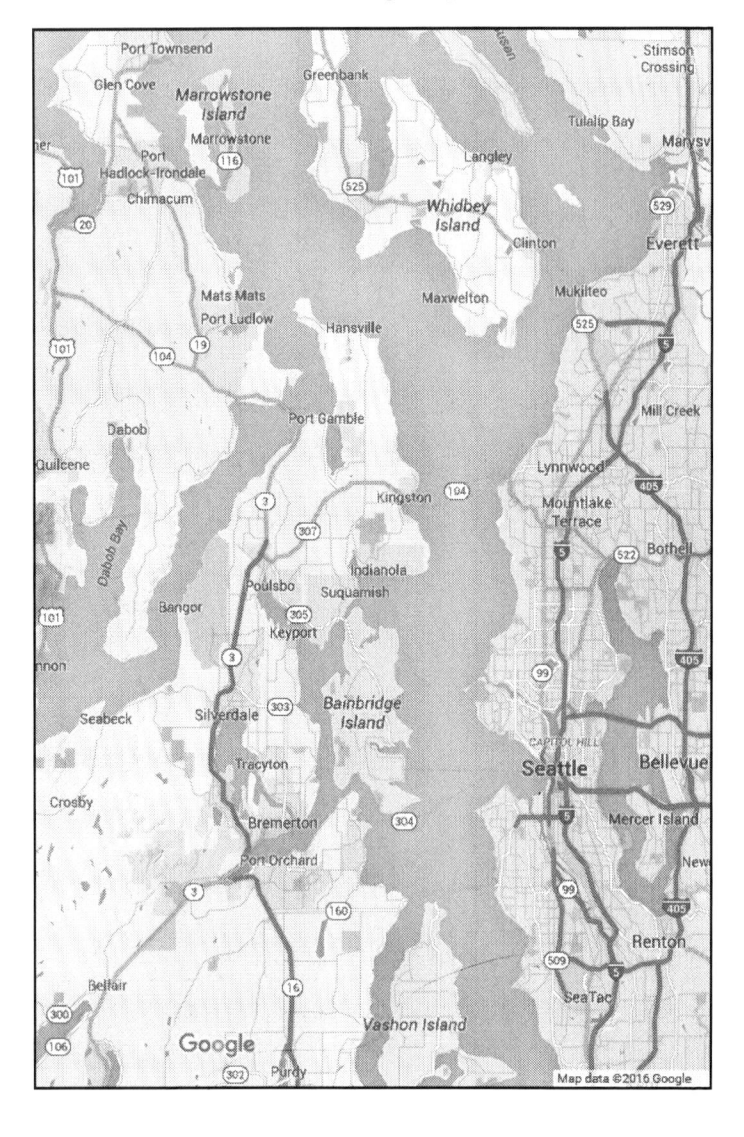

Introduction

WELL EDUCATED and raised as a lady, Betty Bard in 1927 married a man she barely knew. The newlyweds immediately started a chicken ranch in the remote American Northwest. Here Betty had to contend with a difficult husband, loneliness, pregnancy, primitive neighbors, and thousands of chickens. This was the stuff of her first book and the beginnings of a unique writer: in 1945 she published *The Egg and I*, a lightly fictionalized account of her life as a chicken farmer. The book was an immediate success, selling a million copies in less than a year, and was eventually translated into over thirty languages. A Hollywood movie of the book appeared two years later and at least eight further movies based on the popular *Egg and I* characters Ma and Pa Kettle were to follow.

In the decade following, Betty wrote a number of highly popular children's books and three more semi-autobiographical works: *The Plague and I*, about her confinement in a tuberculosis sanatorium, *Anybody Can Do Anything*, about her family's struggles in the Depression, and *Onions in the Stew*, about living on an island in Puget Sound. These four comic memoirs of a life in the West and Northwest range from a rough mining community in Montana to the lush Olympic Peninsula and the bright lights of big city Seattle. Her life may even be viewed as a paradigm of early twentieth-century American experience: pioneering, homesteading, the Great Depression, war, and finally prosperity.

To a great degree Betty's life is in her work, even allowing for its fictional elements and humorous exaggeration. Her writing is used as one of the multiple sources in this book – always clearly labeled as such – because to neglect what Betty wrote about her own life would be to disregard that story's most vital wellspring. Sometimes, though, it's an unreliable voice; she was writing to amuse. Questions remain for every fan of Betty's books. What really happened? What happened to Betty in the end? What became of Betty's family? Drawing from numerous other sources – historical and legal records, private correspondence, interviews, newspapers and journals, local history, contemporary accounts – many of these questions are answered here.

The hard core of older fans continue to read and re-read Betty's work with a deep devotion but she is becoming less well known. Her sharp, sometimes malicious wit, her universally recognizable descriptions of the warmth and quarrels of family life, and the pictures she painted of a more innocent time in the Pacific Northwest are in danger of being lost to future generations of readers.

Some Saturday mornings, as soon as the mountains had bottled up the last cheerful sound of Bob and the truck, I, feeling like a cross between a boll weevil and a slut, took a large cup of hot coffee, a hot-water bottle, a cigarette and a magazine and WENT BACK TO BED. *Then, from six-thirty until nine or so, I luxuriated in breaking the old mountain tradition that a decent woman is in bed only between the hours of seven pm and four am unless she is in labor or dead.*

(The Egg and I)

Betty and Bob

ANNE ELIZABETH CAMPBELL BARD was working on the family farm on the Olympic Peninsula, across from the city of Seattle in America's Pacific Northwest, when one day her younger brother brought home an old acquaintance. Bob Heskett was a former US Marine who had served in the First World War, very tall and very handsome, and Betty was immediately attracted. She had few hopes, however. Betty was plump and unsure of herself and much overshadowed by her manic and wildly popular older sister Mary, a flame-haired siren who attracted all the attention. What Betty did have was a wickedly sharp sense of humor, a great relish for life and a brilliant, wide-spreading smile. To her utter amazement and delight, the seemingly suave Bob appeared to prefer her to Mary.

Mary and her friends were struck dumb by Bob Heskett's dark good looks and white teeth, Betty was to write later in *The Egg and I*, and she was simply bowled over that he liked her and not her older sister. Bob was twelve years older than Betty, and no doubt appeared very sophisticated. He took her out to dinner and the movies and the affair gathered momentum; Betty later confided to a friend that Bob 'seduced' her in the strawberry patch. But even before the strawberry patch incident Bob had already proposed and Betty had tremulously accepted. In 1927 she and Bob were married in a quiet family ceremony at the house of a friend and then departed for a honeymoon in the quaint Canadian city of Victoria, only a short ferry ride from Seattle.

Bob seemed morose and preoccupied on the honeymoon, Betty wrote in *Egg*. If so, he was certainly thinking about one thing in particular: raising chickens.

Beginnings

BETTY'S MOTHER was fair-haired, brown-eyed Elsie Sanderson, an elegant young dress designer from a prosperous New York family. In 1900 the Sandersons were temporarily living in Boston for their children's education and lodging in exclusive Newbury St, a very desirable area then eclipsing even Beacon Hill as a place to live. Many of the big, classically-styled row houses lining the street had all the latest amenities like indoor plumbing and coal-burning furnaces. Some time in those early years of the new century, Elsie happened to be alone at home one day when a student arrived in answer to the family's advertisement for a mathematics tutor to her younger brother Jim, who had already entered Yale while still in his teens. The applicant was a young Harvard man, exactly the same age as Elsie. Unruffled, Elsie proceeded to conduct the interview with the tall and handsome student herself. Darsie Bard got the job. He also reeled home to tell his room-mate that he had met the girl he intended to marry.

Darsie Campbell Bard was from Hannibal, Missouri, born in 1878 and the only child of insurance salesman James Fletcher Bard and his wife Anne Elizabeth. Darsie's mother's family, the Campbells, had originally emigrated to Virginia from Ireland (not Scotland, as Betty wrote in her books); the unusual first name of Darsie appears to have come from George Darsie, the minister husband of Anne Elizabeth's sister Coranelle. Darsie's Kentucky-born father James became a gambler and spent time in jail after embezzling money from his insurance agency employers;

his wife was left to support herself and her son by taking in sewing, teaching school and clerking. On his release, James continued gambling and eventually abandoned his family. Divorce was granted in 1901 on the grounds of desertion and cruelty, and James lived for two more decades before burning to death when his nightclothes caught fire from an open gas stove.

In 1900, when his father was still in evidence and the Bards were living in Portland, Oregon, the young Darsie defied his family's wishes by going East to study. His pioneer parents had wanted him to remain in the West and go to the University of Oregon, but Darsie was determined to study geology at Harvard and so obstinately headed in the opposite direction. He was sporty and adventurous as well as academically gifted, and at Harvard won several prizes in the Metropolitan Regatta and other river races. His only problem was a lack of money. To earn enough to attend his classes he worked all night in the Harvard College Observatory, which meant that getting enough sleep became a pressing problem. Tutoring rich boys might solve the difficulty, he thought, and hence his appearance on the Sandersons' doorstep.

When well-brought-up Elsie first laid eyes on Darsie she could have had no idea she was about to embark on a life of adventure. Elsie was an artist. She had loved to draw and paint all her life and at thirteen, when her brother Jim was ill and seeing frightening animals in his dreams, Elsie had helped him overcome his terrors by making funny drawings of the animals – elephants with fringed backs, and leopards with warts instead of spots. She later decided to illustrate the English writer Lewis Carroll's nonsensical *Jabberwocky* poems for her brother in the same way and then, daringly, sent them to Carroll himself. The writer never received them. He had died while coincidentally en route to America, but Carroll's brother wrote Elsie a note thanking her for the drawings and assuring her that Lewis would have liked them. He also sent them on to a well-known artist friend in Boston. This was Eric Pape, who was impressed enough by Elsie's talent to contact her and encourage her to continue with her art. When he opened the Eric Pape School of Art in Boston in 1898, Elsie studied illustrative technique and fashion design there as one of his first students. (Fellow artists at the school included the famous painters N. C. Wyeth and Gordon Grant.) Eventually she was offered her dress-designing job by a professional couturier after he happened to see some paper doll costumes she had made for young friends.

Now this artistic and talented young woman had met an adventurous young man from a very different background. Darsie and Elsie fell in love and announced their engagement – utterly to the Sandersons' horror, their daughter Betty was to write in *The Egg and I*. Elsie's patrician mother Mary was descended from Dutch ancestors, the Ten Eycks, who had settled in New York in the seventeenth century and later married into the Thalimer family. In Betty's account, Elsie's family are shocked that Elsie would consider a penniless Westerner who was having to *work* his way through Harvard. Betty describes Elsie's mother as a consciously refined woman, proud of her beautiful figure and erect bearing, who throws fits and tantrums about the proposed match. Her equally strong-willed daughter Elsie ignores the histrionics and holds firm.

Plans were finally made for a grand wedding but on 15 December 1902, Elsie Thalimer Sanderson and Darsie Campbell Bard, after a year's engagement, were married quietly in St. Andrew's Church in Boston. Both were twenty-four. Elsie's own account in later life was that this 'sort of elopement' was a way of avoiding the fuss of a big society wedding with hundreds of guests, which would not have been to the young couple's tastes. The marriage was not made public until March the following year, when Elsie's mother, now back in New York and living on Madison Avenue, inserted a notice in the *New York Herald*. She told an interviewer from the paper that Darsie, although still a senior at Harvard, had obtained a good position in Butte, Montana, and in December had learned that he must take it up on the first of the year; he and Elsie therefore decided to marry quietly. The new bride had then immediately departed to visit relatives in Auburn, New York (probably Elsie's maternal grandparents, the Coxes) and the Sandersons themselves only learned of their daughter's marriage when Elsie announced in March 1903 that she was off to join her husband out West. There was a 'period of tears', but all ended happily. 'She is the happiest girl I ever saw,' Mrs Sanderson trilled to the paper, 'and I suppose their little caprice must be forgiven.' She appears to have talked Darsie up somewhat, as the article describes him as being 'from an old and aristocratic Kentucky family'. Darsie's home state of Oregon then picked up the story. The *Oregonian* newspaper declared that the undergraduate body at Harvard had been 'surprised today at the announcement of the secret marriage last December'. Darsie was described as quiet and retiring, and a brilliant scholar.

After the marriage ceremony Darsie immediately left for Butte to start work in a diamond mine. Once settled with somewhere to live, he sent for Elsie, and the young bride departed her cultured surroundings to start married life in what was then a rough mining town. To mark this new beginning she decided to change her name to Sydney, the name of an older brother who had died in childhood and of her father and grandfather, although she altered the original spelling from 'i' to 'y'. She had never liked her own name, and Darsie didn't much like it either. She was known as Sydney for the rest of her life but always signed her paintings E. S. Bard, for Elsie Sydney. She also made another decision: never to worry about house-cleaning. Her mother was an immaculate housekeeper, to the point of fetish, and Sydney vowed she would never make it a priority. A very free and easy atmosphere was the result for the future Bard family.

From that point on, Sydney's life with Darsie was a succession of sudden moves and transplantings all over the United States, including Alaska, and even to Canada. If Darsie's work took him away to isolated areas for a long period, Sydney lived in a hotel room or rented house nearby while he was out in the field. None of the moves found Sydney unwilling or unready. When the children started appearing she merely rounded up however many babies she happened to have at the time, packed hurriedly, and set off into the unknown with her peripatetic husband.

Butte was brash but Sydney found she loved living in the West, Betty was to write later. The color and adventure of life there appealed to her, even though according to Betty she was shocked to find that the ladies of the town painted their faces like harlots. When after a year in Butte she discovered she was pregnant, Sydney was delighted, despite the fact that it meant staying at home while Darsie went off alone. She refused to go back East for the delivery, but as a sop to her distraught family she chose a woman doctor who had trained in Philadelphia (and who turned out to practice homeopathy, which Sydney subsequently adopted).

The first of the Bards' six children, Mary, was born in Butte in 1904. For a middle name she was given the family name of Ten Eyck and so of course, Betty said, she was taunted throughout early schooldays as Mary Tin Neck. When Mary was still a baby Darsie was sent down to the Nevada desert to examine gold deposits and once again Sydney gamely accompanied him, in Betty's account living in a shack and riding a horse with the infant Mary held on the saddle in front of her. The young family next moved to Boulder, Colorado, and here Sydney gave birth to her second child, Betty, after a labor of only two hours.

Darsie's eccentric mother Anne Elizabeth, known to the little ones as Gammy, was now living with the family and was the only one to attend Sydney during the birth because the doctor had been delayed. Betty recounted the family legend that because her grandmother had been 'delicately reared' she thought the umbilical cord had to be tied in a knot and attempted to do so by looping the newborn under and over, before eventually Sydney just sat up and tied it off herself.

Births were not routinely recorded in the area at that time but later census and educational records show Betty's birth to have been on 26 March 1907. The new baby, whose hair was white but later turned red, was named Anne Elizabeth Campbell after Gammy.

When Betty was only a few months old a wire came asking if the family could be ready to move to Mexico for two years by the following week. They were and they did, together with Gammy. Here little red-haired Mary was much admired by the Mexicans and, according to Betty, learned to speak fluent Spanish. Sydney found life in

Mexico fairly peaceful in the main, apart from the odd earthquake, but Darsie was again off on prospecting trips much of the time and there were many problems for the two lone women living in a strange country with very young children. Tiny Betty on one occasion suffered a dangerous case of hives, a kind of skin rash, due to what Sydney suspected was too much formaldehyde in the milk. The unflappable Sydney took it in her stride. If she couldn't find a remedy for the children's ailments in her well-worn home doctoring book she would dose them with calomel (a purgative), milk of magnesia, or the homeopathic medicine aconite. If nothing could be found to treat an illness she would either leave it to nature or, on rare occasions, resort to a simple technique: she would call up a hospital and ask for a list of physicians who treated the condition and then pick the last on the list of names. Her theory was that he would be young and struggling, wouldn't charge too much, and would have the time and patience to make night calls.

After about a year the family moved yet again, to the mining camp of Placerville near Boise in Idaho, a town of fewer than two hundred souls to whom supplies were trekked in by mule train. Betty wrote in *Egg* that the camp was in the mountains and that heavy snows fell in the winter; Sydney had to make sure she always had plenty of food. Sydney did what she could to make their flimsy house livable and in November 1908, after another quick, three-hour labor, she gave birth alone to Betty's red-headed little brother Sidney Cleveland Bard, or just Cleve as he became known. The 'Cleveland' came from Sydney's father's middle name, and there was another Cleveland in Sydney's mother's family. According to Betty there was a certain amount of comment in Placerville about all the red hair, given that Sydney was blonde and brown-eyed and

Darsie was black-haired and gray-eyed, but unbeknownst to others Darsie had a bright red beard if he let it grow. 'I trust you won't feel called upon to have a child in every state in the union,' Sydney's father reportedly wired.

The growing family moved back to Butte when Darsie was appointed Professor of Geology and Mineralogy at the Montana State School of Mines. Here they remained from 1910 to 1916, living at 1039 West Granite St, a clapboard house with gables and a shingled roof. Their new home, perched high above the street, was not far from the School of Mines and just south of the mining railroad which carried ore from the mines to the smelter in Anaconda. Darsie would cross the tracks to get to work, and the rattle of the busy cars and the roar of the dynamite blasting going on below the town punctuated the day for Sydney and the children at home. The mountain of Big Butte loomed over all, marked with a large white M for the Montana School of Mines.

At that time Butte was still one of the largest cities west of the Mississippi, a notorious copper boom town with hundreds of saloons and a famous red-light district variously called 'The Line' or 'The Copper Block', where the hordes of young miners looking for entertainment were sure to find it at any hour of the day. At one end of the scale was the famous Dumas Brothel, one of a number of elegant bordellos in bustling Mercury Street, while at the other was the somewhat less elegant Venus Alley where the women plied their trade in small cubicles called 'cribs'.

The young Betty was doubtless oblivious to all this, probably because Gammy made the children avert their eyes whenever they walked past a saloon, but she did write about the biting cold in winter, the huge icicles which hung outside the windows, and having her frozen cheek thawed with snow by Sydney. She also recalled the lack of grass in their yard. All the topsoil had been washed away during the mining for gold and gems and other minerals which had taken place right in the midst of Butte's residential districts. There was just one handkerchief-sized patch of green in the front yard, Betty wrote, and here she would sit playing with her dolls and trying not to damage the grass.

As a toddler Betty was slow to talk, a wonder to Sydney as the child showed great intelligence in every other way, but when she did finally begin at almost three it was in complete sentences with every word pronounced exactly right. Children who talk late are often extremely bright, and certainly Betty would fit this profile (although with characteristic modesty she referred to herself as an 'outstanding dullard' for this delay in speech). At ages five and four she and Cleve attended a local kindergarten while Mary went to the McKinley School, a redbrick building not far from their home; when Betty turned six, she too started in the first grade at McKinley but was moved to second when it was discovered that she could already read and write. She was paralyzingly shy and never spoke above a whisper, Betty wrote later, and it had taken several months for the teachers to realize her capabilities.

Mary and Betty wore white stockings to school every day and shoes with patent leather bottoms and white kid tops. After school, if the weather was nice, she remembered going outside with an apron over her dress – insisted upon by Gammy – to play on the dump at Darsie's place of work, the Montana School of Mines. Here the children would find lots of the little clay retort cups which had been used for assaying gold. Their games were normally masterminded by Mary, who from an early age was very inventive, Betty said, and had tremendous enthusiasm, especially for her own juicy big ideas which her younger siblings were usually forced to implement. Betty and Cleve were Mary's natural guinea pigs; the younger children proved to be more dubious. These ideas included Mary inventing perpetual motion by getting Betty to hold out a long pole in front of a descending sled with the idea that the pole would then rebound off the wall of their house and push the sled back up the hill again, and so on *ad infinitum* (the experiment knocks out Betty's front teeth); Mary convincing Cleve to walk across a plank suspended over the cellar stairs (he falls off onto the stairs and injures his back); and Mary talking Betty into sliding down an old mining flume in the mountains or jumping from a hayloft onto a pile of straw in which an upturned rake proves to lie hidden.

In Betty's writing about her childhood Mary looms large: where Mary leads, Betty follows, and this continues throughout their adolescence and early adulthood. Even when Betty is a young woman Mary is still persuading her into things she doesn't want to do, whether it's going out with short, dandruffy men for whom Mary has promised to find a date or getting her to interview for a dubious job which combines typing with modeling fur coats. She even harangues Betty into writing her first book, at least the way Betty described it. In Betty's eyes Mary was always the talented one of the family and the wittiest; her friends remembered her repeating Mary's anecdotes and *bons mots,* and Mary's spirited opinions and tirades are peppered throughout Betty's books.

A baby sister, Sylvia Remsen Bard, was born in 1912 or 1913. (The unusual name Remsen probably derived from Sydney's grandmother Mary Remsen Ten Eyck, born in

1821.) Tragically, the baby died at four months from the then untreatable pertussis, or whooping cough, which had set in six weeks earlier; she was one of eleven young children in Butte to die of the deadly disease that year. A family funeral was held at the house and little Sylvia was buried in Butte's Mount Moriah Cemetery. No marker or gravestone remains.

Betty, then aged six, never mentioned this sister and her sad death in her writing. Another little sister, Dorothea Darsie, a dark-haired baby this time, was born in 1915 when Betty was in the second grade at McKinley. The new baby, different in temperament as well as looks, was nicknamed Dede, and according to the family became especially close to her father Darsie. Luckily the new little sister thrived, although that winter was a particularly hard one for the Bards. Betty contracted scarlet fever, and Mary and Cleve had to be sent away to friends to keep them out of danger.

At some point during all this fecundity the ever-creative Sydney had invented a sort of sling for the later stages of pregnancy: made out of heavy unbleached muslin, it was a hammock with tabs that tied around the bump, little darts up the front which made a strong nest for the stomach, and straps over the shoulders to carry some of the weight. In later life she made one for Betty's best friend Blanche, who said it made a big difference and should have been patented.

The family spent some of their summers camping in the mountains, accompanying Darsie on his various expeditions. Family lore has it that when the children were still small, Sydney would tie a rope around their waists and tether them to a stake as she busied herself around the camp. Betty wrote in *Egg* that she dated her 'still smoldering' hatred of wild animals from these trips. They would come across bears and lions on their walks and at night the coyotes and timber wolves would howl dismally outside the tents. If Gammy was along on the trip to look after them the children refused to go anywhere with Sydney and Darsie, who were forever walking logs over dangerous ravines or descending into deep dark mine tunnels or fording furious streams. Gammy, on the other hand, had an instinct for danger and carefully avoided it. The children, and especially Betty, much preferred cowering inside a cabin with their grandmother, out of the reach of 'groping fangs'. They loved tiny, blue-eyed Gammy, in Betty's description an eccentric and pessimistic woman who kept her money in her Bible where she thought it would be safe from burglars, and wore her corsets upside down with the bust part fitting over the hips. She hated all men (except her own son) and was a terrible cook, but she read to her grandchildren indefatigably and let them into her cozy rumpled bed whenever they were lonely or frightened.

Seattle

When Darsie, accompanied by Sydney, went on a mining trip to Mount Baker in northwest Washington State, he fell in love at first sight with nearby Puget Sound and the city of Seattle. Here, he decided, was the place to live. Seattle, green and hilly and overlooking the Sound, was a boom-and-bust city: first lumber, then the Klondike Gold Rush when the city became a hub for the miners in Alaska and the Yukon, and then shipbuilding during World War I. This last boom was still in progress when in 1916 Sydney, Darsie, Gammy and the children, consisting now of Mary, Betty, Cleve and Dede, departed the smoke and fumes of Butte for the verdant spaces of the Pacific Northwest. In Seattle they moved into number 2212 on what has since become Everett Avenue East on Capitol Hill. Darsie started a geological engineering consultancy with his partner J. C. Johnson, quickly finding impressive clients such as the Milwaukee Railroad and the Ladysmith Smelters of Vancouver Island. At the same time he joined professional and graduate clubs which offered social opportunities for his wife and family. In 1918, at the age of forty, he also registered for the draft, although apparently was never called up; perhaps he had a yen for the military, having previously done a brief stint in the Signal Corps of the Oregon National Guard.

The Bards' new house had been owned by the Vice-Consul of Denmark and was fairly grand, with a ballroom in the basement which health-obsessed Darsie turned into a gymnasium. His ideas about health had already been a torment for the children back in Butte. According to Betty's later writing he would make them run round the block each morning before breakfast, even when it was bitterly cold, and now they were made to do the same in Seattle. Salt was not allowed, nor the drinking of water at meals, and each mouthful had to be chewed one hundred times. He bought carloads of apples, made them eat brick-hard toast and raw vegetables, and read aloud long dull articles on natural foods. The older children were also enrolled in the YWCA and YMCA gym and swimming classes, which Betty blamed for her lifelong hatred of exercise. The teachers were invariably 'big mannish women with short hair and sadistic tendencies', she wrote. And, to keep their minds healthy, Darsie did not allow them to read comics or go to the movies. Naturally the children had no wish to be healthy and wanted to go to the movies and read comics like everyone else, so as soon as Darsie left on one of his prolonged mining trips they stopped running around the block and got out the funny papers. Sydney did nothing, as neither she nor Gammy wanted to get up at five in the morning for cold baths and exercises any more than the children did.

Having arrived in Seattle, pioneering was at an end, wrote Betty. In addition to their school lessons she and Mary were embarked upon a program of cultural instruction, perhaps at the instigation of cultivated Sydney: music and dancing lessons, French and drama. Betty claimed that she wasn't very good at piano, despite having long thin hands, and thought she was completely outshone by Mary who couldn't read music and never practiced but in Betty's estimation still managed to play a hundred times better. The girls also received cookery instruction from Sydney herself, who was an accomplished cook. This included the finer aspects of cuisine such as homemade mayonnaise and lighting candles at the dinner table.

In 1918 or 1919, after a year on Capitol Hill, the family moved yet again. Their new house in affluent Laurelhurst, 5120 E 42nd Avenue, was perched high on a bluff above 20-mile-long Lake Washington. The house, old and run-down, was a big Victorian, which eventually stood in sizable grounds after the later purchase of several surrounding lots. There were tennis courts, a vegetable garden, and an orchard, and the family also bought a large collection of animals including a horse and a cow. Inside, in their shared bed, Mary would plant her cold feet on eleven-year-old Betty's back to make her continue the stories she made up about the two orphan sisters Nancy and Plum.

The house at Laurelhurst
Courtesy Puget Sound Regional Archives

The house was constantly filled with pets and friends, Betty wrote in *Egg*. The family now numbered seven, except when Darsie was away, but the table was usually set for twelve and sometimes forty – guests of Darsie's, Sydney's, or Gammy's, plus the children's friends. The younger members of the family were spaced around the table to discourage fighting and were allowed to join in the conversation, but only if they kept to topics of general interest. Guests or not, every night Sydney set the table with candles, silver, glassware and flowers. The Bards were doing well, and judging by Betty's account lived in some style, with maids and a nurse for the younger children.

For the older children there were private schools. Betty and Mary attended the all-girl nonsectarian St. Nicholas School in the wealthy area of Capitol Hill. The school at that time was an imposing structure of classical design on the Hill's main Broadway thoroughfare. Several expensive changes of uniform were required from the upscale

Frederick & Nelson department store, including, for gym classes, black serge bloomers, a white middy blouse and a black tie and stockings. Girls from many of Seattle's leading families were students there; the school prepared them to pursue higher education (many were accepted into prestigious women's colleges such as Wellesley, Vassar, Smith, and Bryn Mawr) and to take their places in the upper echelons of Seattle society. Emphasis was on academics but also on proper behavior, charitable service, cultural activities and the creation of a gracious home. Betty's parents – perhaps Sydney more so than Darsie – clearly wanted their daughters to be educated as young ladies.

Sydney herself was involved in charitable work, and Mary and Betty were now joining in. In August 1919, for example, they were both members of a girls' dancing troupe performing an interpretative dance at a fête in aid of the Seattle Day Nursery Association.

Money appears to have been flowing in, although at a price, as Darsie was still often absent on mining trips for as much as six months in the year. Nevertheless, life seemed very settled for the family in their lively big home above the lake.

Darsie

It was a Sunday afternoon in January 1920; Betty was twelve. Her father was away from home, testifying as an expert witness in a lawsuit back in Butte as he was frequently called upon to do. The children were all involved on various projects around the house and artistic Sydney, pregnant again with her sixth child, was quietly painting a picture.

Suddenly the peace was interrupted by the arrival of an urgent telegram. Darsie was desperately ill with streptococcal pneumonia and Sydney was to come at once. Sydney left for Butte immediately, hurrying downtown to the station to board the Northern Pacific train for a journey of some twenty-one hours.

But in those days, when treatment options were limited, there was little that could be done. Darsie, at the age of only forty-one, died a few days after Sydney's arrival. The obituary in the local newspaper called him 'one of the foremost geologists and mineralogists in the United States', and printed a large etching of Darsie; the Butte Masonic Lodge, where Darsie had been a Mason, held services in his memory. His many old friends and former students in Butte were shocked by his untimely death.

Sydney brought her husband's body home for cremation, making what must have been a terrible, heartbroken train journey back from Montana. She was completely devastated. The younger children were bewildered but fully aware that something had gone tragically wrong with their happy existence.

Sydney's aristocratic mother, Mary Sanderson, came to comfort her daughter and to look after the children. They all hated her snobbish ways and condescending attitude, although Betty wrote that the visit from 'Deargrandmother', as she made them call her, did help to take their minds off the tragedy. Eventually she went back East and for the most part life continued for the children much as before, used as they were to Darsie's frequent absences. For Sydney, of course, it was much harder. At some point during the months after Darsie's death Sydney one morning refused to get out of bed. Mary, the eldest, went to her bedside and pleaded with her, telling her that the family needed her and that she just had to get up. Sydney forced herself to rise and get dressed – there was no choice. She had four children to care for and another about to come into the world. In June she gave birth to her last child, red-haired baby Alison.

Family life resumed, if much changed, and in time Sydney even took up her previous charitable and social activities. In April she had been among the patronesses of an event held by the Wellesley Club of Western Washington to raise funds for scholarships, and in later years she would be mentioned in the *Seattle Times* as giving a tea for an old friend from Butte (assisted by 'the Misses Mary and Betsy Bard'), or with her daughters helping at a Laurelhurst Guild tea in aid of the Children's Orthopedic Hospital. She never remarried. In the years to come people would sense the great love and admiration with which she always spoke of handsome, adventurous Darsie.

In her books Betty doesn't dwell on her father's death. She wrote only that the year following his death was a very sad one. Their father had often been absent, sometimes for months on end, and when he was at home he had put his reluctant offspring through rigid diets, enforced calisthenics and cold baths at five in the morning. His scientific mind had also led him to administer tests to the children for color blindness and other conditions when they were only babies, and to give them intelligence tests as soon as they could talk, but perhaps all of this came from love and concern as much as scientific inquiry. Darsie's dreadful obsession with health, for instance, was because Betty in particular was a frail child who caught every illness going, although she only learned this later in life. And despite his mania for health and experiments in child-rearing Darsie had been an outgoing, sociable man – often inviting people to stay with the family for months on end – who had a good sense of humor.

He was certainly amused in the face of his children's unwillingness to adopt his various regimes. When he instituted the early-morning cold baths for the children, for instance, Betty wrote that he had at first put them on their honor; they cheated, naturally, and Darsie gave them a week as he listened to their pretend screams in the bathroom before buying some horribly coarse towels and personally drying them off after full immersion in the freezing water. When he taught them sportsmanship as part of their Saturday tennis lessons, insisting they jump the net after the game and shake hands, Betty could see that he took their accompanying stuck-out tongues and pretend vomiting in good part. The children may have hated the early baths and the exercises but Darsie was also a father to be loved.

Now this larger-than-life parent was gone. His death changed their lives in one other important respect. Money became tight, and got tighter. A technicality in Darsie's will meant that the family had absolutely no money coming in and Sydney had to go to court to secure funds from his estate merely in order to live. She successfully petitioned for almost all of it to be invested in bonds at 7% interest per annum, maturing after five years. She then entered into a complicated financial agreement with an old friend of Darsie's with whom he had co-owned a Montana mine, receiving an initial payment but not the profit that was eventually due to her. The family's income plummeted.

All the extracurricular lessons except piano and ballet ceased, and the older children were switched to public schools from the fall of 1920. Once again the children had to adjust to a new environment. As an adult Mary had a theory that all the moving around as children meant that the Bard offspring were continually having to adapt to new places, new climates, new friends and new schools, and that this was never hard for the Bards because they all had plenty of vitality and excellent health and liked to adjust. This sounds more like Mary just describing Mary. After Darsie's death the sudden change of schools, loss of friends, and straitened circumstances are likely to have affected shy and sensitive Betty far more profoundly.

Darsie's disciplined ways were also swept aside and Betty wrote that the children began to do exactly what they wanted, including staying with friends for weeks on end without telling their mother. Sydney's only stipulation for the behavior of her brood, apart from good manners and not sulking, was never to tell a lie.

Growing up

Betty described herself at about age twelve as extremely thin and with braces on her teeth. She was completely overshadowed by the highly popular Mary, who went off to parties and brought hordes of boys to the house. Betty stayed home, playing with the younger children and washing the dishes with a sore heart. She was to write that in the school yearbook Mary was labeled Torchy, 'the girl who put the pep in pepper', while under poor Betty's picture was 'An honor roll student – a true friend'. When Mary started winning elocution contests with her high-drama performances she offered to coach Betty, who was delirious with happiness because she thought Mary's stomping renditions were simply marvelous. Despite

Betty's thinness and braces Mary decided she was the 'cute' type, which Betty realized in later years was either kindness or wishful thinking, but in any case it gave her more confidence. Taught by Mary, she wrote that she too attempted some recitals, sticking out her lips in a pout and waggling her finger and lisping her way through the pieces. The family were completely nauseated, but some of her schoolfriends liked it and Betty was tempted to take up elocution herself but was (perhaps luckily) unable to do so because of the family finances.

Then came adolescence. Suddenly Betty was no longer thin but rosily plump, with a curvy figure:

I grew a large, firm bust and a large, firm stomach and that was not the style. The style was my best friend, who was five feet ten inches tall and weighed ninety-two pounds. She had a small head and narrow shoulders and probably looked like a thermometer, but I thought she was simply exquisite. I bought my dresses so tight I had to ease into them like bolster covers and I took up smoking and drinking black coffee...

Betty found this sudden swelling a 'bitter thing' and tried various diets but to no avail. She also started getting taller, eventually growing to a height of nearly 5' 7", but she was to return to being painfully thin at other stages in her life. Meanwhile, Mary got all the boys and Betty got the high marks.

It was not all adolescent angst. Betty's new public school was Lincoln High, where in 1921 she twice appeared on the school's honor roll. A friend of the family, Margaret Bundy, recalled that Mary and Betty instantly made new friends, taking them home to Laurelhurst so that the old house rang ever more loudly with the noise of young people. Sunday evening open house at the Bards' became an institution, with dancing to music from the phonograph, fires on the beach and swimming in the lake. Sydney, sometimes called just 'Syd', became a second mother to her young visitors. Margaret could see that Mary had a 'wayward streak' in her and was made aware that she had been prone to tantrums. These had been held in check by Darsie while he was alive but not by Sydney, who in Margaret's opinion wanted her children to like her and would smoke and drink with them as they grew into adolescence. Called 'Mother' before their father's death, they now called her by her first name.

At Lincoln Betty made a particularly good friend, Blanche Hamilton, who remained close to Betty and the Bard family throughout Betty's life. As Blanche Caffiere she wrote '*Much Laughter, A Few Tears*', an account of their schooldays and longstanding friendship. Blanche was fascinated by Betty from the first moment she saw her. She wrote that Betsy, as she was still known at that point, had reddish-brown hair, hazel eyes, and gold braces on her teeth at a time when braces were unusual. She wore a round comb in her hair which she constantly played with when she wasn't waving her hand in the air during Miss Taggart's Latin class. She often wore a blue chambray dress, Norfolk-style (pleated and belted), with a black patent leather belt laced through panels. Betty confided to Blanche that this was her uniform from her former private school St. Nicholas. Money was no doubt too short for new clothes. Blanche noted that Betty wasn't the sporting type – she never turned out for games at Lincoln High and couldn't hold a bat to save her life.

The two girls were assigned lockers next to each other and Blanche began to enjoy Betty's company when they met at the lockers between classes. One day as they were putting their books away a girl with disheveled brown hair and wire-rimmed glasses stopped by and made a remark. The remark was not meant to be funny, but that and the girl's appearance amused them both in the same way and they could hardly wait for the girl to pass by before bursting into giggles. Betty said, 'You know, don't you, that she combs her hair with an egg beater?' Instantly Betty and Blanche discovered that they laughed at exactly the same things, and the friendship was sealed. They continued allies throughout their high school years, sometimes getting into trouble because of their shared sense of humor. Everything Betty said struck Blanche as funny, and Betty seemed to feel the same about Blanche.

Even as a young girl Betty was always interested in the minutiae of people's lives and right from the start she wanted to know every little thing about Blanche and her family. Hearing that Blanche's brother Ralph had a knack for getting into trouble, she immediately wanted to know the details, and listened eagerly to Blanche telling about his escapades. Finally, one day coming up to Halloween, Betty told Blanche that her mother would love to hear the stories about Ralph and asked Blanche to come home with her – the first of Blanche's many visits to the eccentric Bard family, whom the adolescent Blanche recognized as special from the very first. All through high school she was to consider an invitation to the Bards' house an assurance of a good time.

Writing her memoir at the age of eighty-five, Blanche seemingly remembered that first visit so well that she could give a detailed account. The girls took the Wallingford streetcar, transferring to the Laurelhurst bus at 45th and University Way. Then, as now, Laurelhurst was a 'posh' place to live and Blanche felt she was being socially upgraded just by riding on the bus. The vehicle wound around the Laurelhurst hills until it reached the end of the line. Here there were no paved streets, only open fields and the Bards' cow tied to a stake and grazing underneath knobby fruit trees. On a little knoll stood the family's old Victorian house. Mrs Bard – or Sydney, as she asked both young and old to call her – met them at the door: tall and thin, with patrician features, smartly plain in dress and extremely warm and charming to her young guest. In the big country kitchen reigned Betty's grandmother Gammy, wearing a white apron with a limp bottom ruffle, and the little white boudoir cap which older women wore in those days to save combing out their long hair early in the morning. The door to Gammy's small bedroom was open, showing the rumpled bed with all her treasures strewn about just as Betty was to describe in her books.

In the spacious dining room Blanche was enchanted to see an enormous oval dining table set with a sizable Halloween favor at each place – jack-o'-lanterns, witches on broomsticks, owls, and black cats. These came from Augustine and Kyer, a pricey upmarket Seattle grocery store located at 1st and Cherry downtown (seemingly items that Sydney had not cut down on). At the meal Sydney sat at the head of the table and used an ornate carving set to serve up a delicious meal of fried chicken, mashed potatoes and gravy off beautiful Wedgwood platters. On that first visit of Blanche's Mary arrived a little late with an unexpected friend in tow, but another place was soon set and the guest made welcome. Gammy ate in the kitchen on the breadboard because, she claimed, it was more peaceful. There was a great deal of talking and laughing round the table and Betty got Blanche to tell everyone her stories about her brother.

Immediately after dinner some boys arrived for Mary and her friend, which made both Betty and Blanche feel a little crestfallen and overwhelmed by Mary's popularity;

rather than pins from boys (a dating custom at the time), all they had were their Honor Society pins from school. But Betty resumed her role as genial hostess and invited Blanche upstairs to see the contents of her big sister's wardrobe. She pulled open the sliding doors of the closet to reveal an array of long party dresses in a variety of colors and, taking a pink one off the hanger, she urged her friend to try it on. Blanche had never worn a formal before, and she quickly slipped out of her navy blue school clothes and slithered into the shimmering satin garment. Betty chose a yellow one for herself and the two girls preened about in front of the full-length mirror, their heavy school shoes poking out underneath the dresses. Caught up in the party mood, Betty suggested phoning a boy whose father let him drive their car and who could bring along a friend. Blanche, who had never had a date, let alone one dressed in a pink formal, stood in utter amazement as these plans for a real date actually materialized. In a few minutes a big Franklin car stopped at the house and Betty and Blanche got into the back seat while in the front, completely oblivious to the girls' gorgeous gowns under their school coats, the two boys discussed the various instruments on the dashboard. The four headed to the University District and drove up and down University Way, or the 'Ave', as it was called, after its initial incarnation as 14th Avenue. Daringly, Betty suggested a drive to a dinner-dancing roadhouse a few miles north of the city limits. Here Ted, the young driver, confined himself to cruising into the roadhouse's circular drive and then straight back out onto the main highway, but technically they had been to a roadhouse and Blanche was thrilled.

Blanche stayed the night and, as the two lay trying to get to sleep in ivory-painted twin beds, in burst Mary.

Bright-eyed and glowing, her copper-colored hair falling onto her shoulders, she announced that she had just been kissed. Blanche remembered feeling some shock at this admission, unusual for the times, but also that she admired Mary's openness. Betty became so exhilarated over the progress of Mary's romance that she declared she wasn't one bit sleepy and wanted to go downstairs to make a batch of fudge. There really were no limits to the entertainment her friend was providing, Blanche thought – formals, boys, a car, a roadhouse, and now midnight fudge. As they were rattling pans and getting out the milk from the icebox, Gammy appeared in her nightdress, not to complain, as Blanche first feared, but to lend a hand. The girls took the fudge up to bed and fell asleep sticky-fingered and surfeited with sugar.

After only a few hours of slumber, Betty shook Blanche awake so that they would make the school bus. The girls had a hurried breakfast, picked up their untouched schoolbooks and flew out to the waiting bus. When Blanche timidly asked what about their homework, Betty replied lightly that they'd do it right there and then. Concentrating with difficulty, and comparing answers, Blanche managed to finish one task by the time they had to transfer to the streetcar. Once on the wooden seats of the Wallingford car the girls began on their Latin assignment, but Betty blithely told Blanche not to bother writing her translations down: they could keep it in their heads and raise their hands a lot for what they knew, and then they wouldn't get called on for what they didn't. Blanche began to understand why Betty's hand was raised so much right at the start of every class.

Another of Blanche's visits to the Bards saw the girls taking a nude midnight swim in the lake – and getting surprised by some boys whom Betty deflected with the suggestion that the boys go home to fetch their swimwear, thus enabling the girls to make their escape. Blanche thought Betty wouldn't mention the lack of swimsuits to Sydney on their return, but she did, to which Sydney simply replied: 'Of course I thought you would do that, so much more fun.' She served them a warming feast of hot chocolate with marshmallows and waffles with maple syrup, everything homemade, and then little Dede and Alison made an appearance in long white nighties with their little toes peeking out from under the bottom ruffle. Blanche recalled that Dede at this point had round, shiny gray eyes, smooth ivory skin and dark brown hair; tiny Alty, a little over two years old, had reddish hair, beautiful amber-colored eyes and the same lovely satin skin as Dede. The little girls each sang a song before toddling back upstairs to bed. Betty was always to love tiny children and on a return visit to Blanche's family she told stories to Blanche's nieces and nephews, making up her own tales for them with a fine sense of just what would amuse each age – a harbinger of the success of the *Mrs. Piggle-Wiggle* and *Nancy and Plum* stories she would later write for children.

When Lincoln High School became crowded, a new school, Roosevelt High, was built just north of the University District. When the impressively built Roosevelt opened in 1922-23, Blanche and Betty moved to the new school as juniors and once again they shared some of the same classes. Their botany teacher, Miss Tomlinson, had a roly-poly figure and long black hair piled high on top of her head – a model for Betty's character *Mrs. Piggle-Wiggle*, Blanche often thought in years to come. Both Betty and Mary were totally unafraid of the teachers and principal and everyone admired the way they spoke up when they didn't like something. Blanche recalled Betty telling a teacher that an algebra assignment he had handed out was too long for springtime, and to everyone's surprise the teacher agreed and shortened the assignment. The class applauded and Betty was the heroine of the hour.

During her high school years Betty shone academically, although her favorite subject was art. Her creativity at this stage expressed itself mostly in this way, though she did write a few juvenile stories. She continued to hate sport but became a reasonable ballet dancer and took part in a number of class recitals, despite having what she described as 'stiff and unpliable' bones and what seemed like fewer joints than everyone else. Both she and Mary attended the Cornish School of Music (now the Cornish College of the Arts). Founded by Nellie Centennial Cornish, known affectionately to her pupils as Miss Aunt Nellie, the school offered music, drama, the visual arts and dance. Mary and Betty both studied under the famous ballerina Mary Ann Wells, many of whose pupils went on to major national and international careers. Mary became proficient and took part in a number of public performances, including a 'Ballet Artistic' at the Metropolitan Theater in 1919, which the Cornish School asked to have judged by professional standards. She was also the Pied Piper of Hamelin in a pageant on Laurelhurst Golf Links in 1920 (Dede played one of the following children) and an Amazon in a Lincoln High School musical in 1922. Betty wrote that Mary dragged her along to perform whenever she could, although Betty's name does not appear on cast lists with the same regularity as Mary's. She remembered once stepping out from a giant grandfather clock to do a scarf dance and another time appearing in the dancing chorus of an opera.

Mary certainly got plenty out of life. She was not only a talented dancer but also a winner of piano competitions, and very active in school business: as Chairman of Lincoln High's committee in charge of club social affairs she took part in bake sales for charity and was a delegate to a High Schools conference. At home she did more work for charities, and plenty of socializing – in 1921 she was reported in the *Seattle Times* as hosting a 'beach supper and dance' at her Laurelhurst home for a friend. Betty seems to have been far less outgoing, less involved in extra-curricular activities and by her own admission far more of a homebody.

In her graduating class picture in Roosevelt's 1924 yearbook, Betty is smiling and attractive, her face framed by her characteristic bangs. Her nickname was 'Bard' (her friend Blanche's was 'Botch'). As a member of the Senior Dance, Vaudeville and Freshman Entertainment Committees and the Glee Club, Betty at Roosevelt appears to have been more interested in performance than academic achievement, despite her former appearances on the honor roll at Lincoln High and membership of the Honor Society at Roosevelt. Elsewhere in the yearbook Blanche appears as a member of the *Roosevelt News* business staff and as one of a select few on the Senior Honor Roll; Betty appears only as understudy for a role in the school's production of a popular farce in the winter of 1923. She is not listed among the aspiring journalists on the *Roosevelt News*, nor among the student artists contributing to the designing and coloring of Christmas cards and illustrations for the yearbook. Her stated ambition in the yearbook, nevertheless, was to be an illustrator (or a wallpaper designer, she also told her family).

High school days were over.

§

In the fall of that same year Betty started at the University of Washington, majoring in art, which according to Betty consisted solely of drawing from plaster casts. She also took classes in English, Spanish, and physical education. It was at this point, when she entered college, that she changed her nickname Betsy to Betty, as she thought it sounded more adult. Later she told Blanche she wished she hadn't. Mary too had attended the University of Washington, taking courses in music, English, French, public speaking, and business administration, before reluctantly withdrawing to help support the family. For the Bards, money was still a problem.

Legend has it that during their college years Mary and Betty used to perform an unnerving double act when driving the family car, an old Franklin. Mary was nearsighted but liked to drive, whereas Betty loathed it, so Mary at the wheel operated the brake and the gear shift while Betty beside her warned of approaching pedestrians and traffic signals.

Round about this time Sydney started a business, a tearoom called the 'Mandarin' on the ground floor of a small apartment building on 15th Avenue NE, somewhat off the University District's main thoroughfare. All the family were involved, Sydney as cook, Mary as hostess and Betty as waitress. Sydney being such a wonderful cook the food was excellent, and for a time the tearoom did very well, receiving a number of mentions in the *Gossip of the Shops* column of the *Seattle Times*. These pieces, possibly written by a friend, enthused about the tearoom's dear little green tables and decorative touches of lacquer red, and Mrs. Bard's salads and sandwiches. But Sydney had been the generous hostess in her own home for too long and was no businesswoman. Too often she would refuse to take any money from the many friends and acquaintances or friends of the children who came to eat there. 'Oh Joe,' she would say, 'let's make this one on me.' After less than a year there was also a relocation to a place on University Way NE where there was a piano for the customers to play, and then another to the ground floor of an old rooming house back where they had started on 15th Avenue NE. The tearoom stopped making money, if it ever had, and when a meat supplier filed a court complaint against Sydney for non-payment, the sheriff impounded the Bards' old Franklin touring car. Sydney signed the car over to the meat company and the action was dismissed, but the 'Mandarin' had to close down. The business had failed.

Money troubles were abounding, in fact. At the time of Darsie's death the family owned their Laurelhurst property outright, but Sydney's subsequent mortgaging and remortgaging for cash kept the family in hot water for the next two decades. So did further business ventures. In 1926 the Bards came across a picturesque farm while driving around the Olympic Peninsula, the scenic region which faces Seattle across Puget Sound. They were all much taken with the place, which was on Beaver Valley Road on the side of the peninsula opposite the city. Betty's brother Cleve, tall, red-haired and restless, loved animals and everything about the outdoors. Never academically minded, he had often played truant from high school and now, only seventeen and with no experience, he appears to have been the driving force behind the Bards' decision to buy the property and try their hand at farming. With the exception of Mary who was living and working in Seattle, the whole family moved to the new property from their big Victorian house in Laurelhurst, which they later rented out. By this time Betty had given up on university, most probably for financial reasons. She had left after the fall semester of 1925, and now started working on the farm along with the others.

The farm comprised some 650 acres. A large herd of cows, a team of horses, flocks of chickens, and goats and pigs came with the property. The Bards' menagerie at Laurelhurst had been handled by a hired boy, but they all loved animals and at first found they enjoyed both the farming and the hordes of friends who came over every weekend to enjoy the butter and cream and eggs they produced. When not entertaining their many guests they all worked hard at the new venture, although occasionally Sydney would stop and find the time to produce beautiful paintings of the surrounding countryside. Dede and Alison were still young and attended a local school.

However, conditions were primitive and isolated, perhaps far more so than they had anticipated in their comfortable home in Seattle. There was as yet no electricity in the area and horses were still used for transportation and farm work. It was hard labor from dawn to dusk. Then, money troubles once again overwhelmed the family. Sydney may not have been meeting payments, and the mortgage on the farm was in any case a complicated affair involving a number of other people; in August 1927 foreclosure proceedings were initiated, and in January of the following year the farm was auctioned off on the steps of the local courthouse.

The Bards may later have played down the actual reason for the loss of the farm, blaming a heavy drainage bill from the county and also the loss of their dairy herd on the discovery of tuberculosis. At the time of purchase they had been assured that their herd of cows had all been tested for tuberculosis and were disease-free, but when a government agent visited the farm it transpired that the cows had not been tested at all. Checks revealed that fourteen of their best milkers seemed to have the disease and would have to be destroyed.

The family salvaged what they could, and made a move to a smaller farm on Center Valley Road which had an old-fashioned farmhouse with only an outhouse for sanitation. Here their income had to depend chiefly on the produce of a flock of about 250 chickens. To supplement this, Mary, who often visited for long periods from Seattle, started a children's dancing class in nearby Port Townsend.

Betty usually made a joke of everything when recounting the trials of life to her friends, but not when the government shot the cows. Betty's old school friend Blanche commented that this was one occasion when Betty wasn't laughing. In fact it was discovered that a mistake had been made in condemning the cows and reparations followed, but in the end the farming venture failed and the Bards acknowledged defeat. Some time between April and fall 1930 they gave up and returned to Seattle to a new house on 15th Avenue. By this time Laurelhurst, too, had been lost. In December 1928 their lovely old home, bought by Darsie so optimistically a decade before, had also been sold on the steps of a courthouse to pay off Sydney's mortgage debts. At least there was some good news: the Montana mine co-owned by Darsie had proved very profitable and, after a lawsuit brought by Sydney, the co-owner agreed to pay a good sum to each of the Bard children.

But before that, when the family was still farming, Betty's brother Cleve had one day bumped into his old acquaintance Bob Heskett in Seattle and invited him home for the weekend. The stage was set.

Betty and the Chickens

BETTY'S NEW HUSBAND, Robert Eugene Heskett, was an ex-Marine and former rancher. Born in 1895 in Cedar Falls, Iowa, he was the eldest of four children. In 1910 Bob's father moved the family to Montana, where for the next seven years Bob worked outdoors on wheat and cattle ranches; according to Betty in *The Egg and I,* he also attended agricultural college and worked as a supervisor on a chicken ranch. In 1916 Bob registered for the draft, giving his occupation as farmer. He served in the US Marines but, presumably after seeing action abroad in the First World War, was medically discharged in 1919 with shell shock (now more commonly termed Post Traumatic Stress Disorder.) After his discharge Bob moved to Seattle to live with his parents and joined his father in selling insurance, which may not have been much to his obviously outdoor tastes. By the time he was romancing Betty he was probably already dreaming of returning to life on a ranch.

Bob and Betty's wedding took place on Sunday 10 July 1927 and was conducted by the Reverend Dr. Herbert Gowen, an Episcopalian priest and father of friends of the Bards – the Bards were nominally Episcopalian, but not particularly religious. The ceremony was held at the Gowens' own house and Bob's parents Otis and his second wife were the witnesses. There is no record of any of the Bards being present, which may suggest an elopement and possibly even a very early pregnancy, perhaps resulting from the strawberry patch incident. Equally, the Bards may simply have disapproved, even though Sydney subsequently announced the marriage in the *Seattle Times*. Mary reportedly loathed Bob Heskett, despite his film star looks, which she compared to movie cowboy Gary Cooper's.

Betty was twenty (but described herself in her writing as younger, only eighteen), and probably fairly inexperienced. She was also very bright, very fond of art and reading, and used to the noise and sociability of a large and bookish family. Now she was about to depart this lively and cultured atmosphere to start married life with a much older man, one she barely knew.

After what seems to have been quite a dull honeymoon with a morose Bob in Victoria, British Columbia, at least as described by Betty in *The Egg and I*, Bob went back to selling insurance for the Mutual Life Insurance Company. By now, though, his fervid intention was to try his hand at chicken farming, a popular enterprise in Washington State in that era. In *Egg* Bob tells Betty that he thinks wheat-farming is hard and thankless but speaks of his chicken-raising days with evident pleasure. The young Betty feels it is her duty, as taught to her by Sydney, to support her new husband in his ambitions. This had certainly worked out for Sydney, who had had a wonderful time following her mining engineer husband all over the US. Betty's own wishes, if she has any, don't appear to come into it, and she falls wholeheartedly in with Bob's plans.

In the book Betty writes about the first time they go to see the property for sale on the Olympic Peninsula that Bob has his eye on for their fledgling farm. She describes a ferry ride across the beautiful Puget Sound towards the snowy Olympic Mountains and the landing at 'Docktown', which from her detailed description is clearly the sawing and logging town of Port Ludlow, at that time connected by ferry to Seattle. In her account they then drive for several hours up into the mountains to inspect the tiny, lonely farm, surrounded by mighty fir trees and looking forlorn as it cowers under the vast Olympics.

Her first impressions from afar are of a sad property that has been abandoned, the buildings weathered and the orchard overgrown, the fences falling down and the windows in the little farmhouse sagging open. She describes a sense of gloom as she gazes at the nearby mountains, so seemingly close that they give her the feeling of someone reading over her shoulder. But once in the farm clearing itself she can see the flowers and blossoming trees and the place seems less sinister, more ready to make friends. Perhaps with a lick of paint and some new windows the old place might actually work, thinks Betty. There are various outbuildings, and the house itself, an old log cabin, is well situated on a rise of ground under which a mature orchard slopes gently down to a large pond fed by a fresh spring. Inside the house there is an enormous square kitchen with a large pantry, a living room, a wood room, and a downstairs bedroom. Two more tiny slope-ceilinged bedrooms are at the top of a creepy flight of stairs. There is no bathroom, only an outhouse. A large, surly-looking rusty stove hulks against one side of the kitchen; old newspapers dating from the 1880s are tacked onto the walls. The place is otherwise empty.

The house faces south across the orchard to the pond and towards the ever-present mountains. Whichever way she turns Betty describes being brought up short against something dense and imposing, and wham! there's another mountain icily ignoring her, as she puts it. But the more they explore the old place the more Betty has the feeling that they should move in and help the little farm in its struggle with the wilderness. Bob is delighted and they decide to snap the place up. They can just about afford to pay cash for the farm and to put enough in the bank for the chickens and feed. Fuel and water, from the trees that surround the farm and the spring by the pond, will be free, and they decide that with a large vegetable garden, pigs to eat leftovers and a few chickens to provide eggs just for themselves they will be able to manage.

In *The Egg and I* the first spring and summer are occupied with just getting the previously derelict farm into some kind of shape. Slowly they make progress, and by the time fall is in the air Bob and Betty have built the chicken houses; plowed, harrowed and planted the garden and a back field (with a horse, not machinery); cleared the orchard of stumps; and bought and installed several hundred yeeping baby chicks. Only now does Bob allow them to start on the lesser matter of the house, which lacks both doors and windows and other such little necessities. There has been frequent rain, and mildew has been forming on the clothes in the closets. The bedclothes are so clammy when they get into bed at night that it's like being covered in seaweed, Betty writes. Now, finally, they lay floors, put in windows, fix broken sills and sagging doors and put in a sink (without water but with a drain). It begins to feel like home. The kitchen still has the malignant stove, anthropomorphized in Betty's beady eye as 'Stove', which had been there when they moved in. This room becomes the hub of all of their activities – keeping egg records, writing checks, making out mail orders, reading letters, eating, washing, taking baths and entertaining. They begin the day in it at four in the morning and end it at about eight-thirty by shutting the damper in the stove and blowing out the kerosene lamp.

They trade their car for a Ford pick-up truck and, in place of various useless wedding presents that would have needed non-existent electricity, they acquire a dragsaw, gasoline lanterns, kerosene lamps and sad irons, which worked by being heated up on the fire. They buy tin washtubs and a pressure cooker. They hew a road into the virgin timber at the back of the ranch and drive the truck out there to saw up fallen cedars and firs with their new dragsaw. Tackling these rough tasks, Betty writes that she quickly learned new ways:

I learned the inadequacy of 'Oh, dear!' and 'My goodness!' and the full self-satisfying savor of sonofabitch and bastard rolled around the tongue.

All of this backbreaking activity is relayed by Betty in *Egg* with her trademark acidic observation and self-deprecation. She paints a picture of herself at this time as pretty green in the ways of farming but at least blessed with abundant energy and very willing to do hard labor as Bob's inept new underling. On moving to the ranch with Bob she immediately loses her status as blushing and fragile bride and becomes merely her husband's sidekick and all-round handyman. Bob is described as snapping and roaring and laughing callously as he belts out commands to a trembling Betty, who begins to realize that she is now just a wife to be ordered around. Much of this is for humorous effect, of course, but Bob is clearly in the driving seat. Romance appears to have fled. Betty does her best to get used to it and to acquire the skills she now needs, and Bob can also be kind and encouraging; he has the right kind of disposition and experience for this kind of work, Betty writes, whereas all she has to offer is her willingness and youthful muscle. That first spring and summer at the ranch she feels both joy and despair as slowly they get the farm up and running.

Even after the house is more fixed up, Betty's life remains one of constant drudgery. There is no sharing of household chores with Bob, and no running water. She carries up ninety-nine per cent of the water for washing clothes into the cabin herself. The water is hard and won't soap properly and after a day scrubbing clothes in the greasy scum Betty writes that she can peel the skin off her hands like gloves. She fails to understand why the other mountain women gain such a sense of accomplishment from a big wash; as far as Betty is concerned she would feel more of a sense of accomplishment if someone else did it while she stayed in bed. The effort to wash and iron in such primitive conditions seems to her entirely futile. Washing herself is just as difficult; she and Bob can take baths only twice a week, in a washtub, when the stove is hot enough to heat the water. They are both tall and find washing in such a tiny receptacle difficult. Betty is still wearing her hair long and hair-washing is another problem.

Ironing is done with the sad irons, which were intentionally heavy and flat in order to get the creases out ('sad' being an old word for heavy). She uses two of them, alternating a detachable handle between each; one heats on the stovetop while the second is in use on the clothes. When the first cools down, the handle is transferred to the now hotter iron on the stove. According to Betty the irons are always covered in black from the stove and merely succeed in dirtying the clean laundry.

Betty also has to trim the kerosene lamps by hand and scrub the wooden floors, which are made of white pine planks carefully laid by Bob, and impossible to keep clean. The floors need constant work once the rainy season sets in and as far as Betty is concerned the whole thing is a waste of time and effort which she greatly resents. She would gladly cover them over with cheap linoleum, but Bob likes the floors and so Betty carries out a daily scrub, which has to be thorough. Bob's insistence on keeping the floors as they are is a cause of marital strife, and she writes that despite her efforts with every kind of cleaning implement the floors always look as if she and Bob spend all their time butchering animals.

In the spring and summer the hard work on the ranch is enlivened with the occasional visit to town, which for the increasingly lonely Betty is a very welcome return to something approaching life. She misses her family and is thrilled to go into the stores and meet other farmers and local townspeople and 'Indians', even if, as she remarks, all the stores smell like sweat and manure. In winter Bob goes into town for supplies on his own, because Betty, desperate as she is for the liveliness of the little town, needs to stay home to look after the chickens and get the gasoline lanterns lit in the chicken houses at the first sign of dusk. Sometimes she even stands a while among the busy chickens in their well-lit abode, which to her feels like a friendly cocktail lounge, just to relieve some of the loneliness. It's ecstasy to hear Bob's returning truck after a long rainy day all on her own, and utter joy in the evening to eat, smoke, and read letters and magazines aloud to each other.

§

Every reader of *Egg* is thoroughly beguiled by Betty's funny, endearing story of a hapless young city woman battling loneliness and hardship as she learns to become the wife of a chicken farmer.

In reality, however, Betty was not as isolated as she said she was.

The distance from Port Ludlow ('Docktown') to Chimacum, the little town close to Bob and Betty's place, was only about ten miles rather than the several hours' drive described in the book, and the area is a broad agricultural valley with the surrounding mountains some way off. In *Egg* the farm is also described as five miles from any neighbor whereas in fact the Bishop family, the prototypes for the book's famous Kettle characters, lived less than a mile away. In addition, although Betty describes feeling lonely and isolated and pining for her family back in civilized Seattle, the rest of the Bards were actually still living on the family farm only a few miles away. Both farms were on the Swansonville Road, not far from Chimacum, with Bob and Betty at number 711. The Bards moved back to the city only in 1930, so in real life Betty must have had her family pretty much next door for the majority of her time on the ranch.

Depicting a more severe isolation, of course, makes for a better story. Betty's books are usually described as autobiographical or semi-autobiographical, and readers have tended to take the detail at face value; but, along with the exaggeration of both her isolation and the nearness of the mountains – a massive, gloomy presence in *Egg* – there are other departures in the book from the real facts of Betty's life. She was not, as she presented herself, a city girl from Seattle, a sophomore in college unused to country ways; when she married Bob she had been working on the family farm for over a year and by then must have been well versed in farm life. Bob was not the cheerful, hard-working husband she painted him – more of this later.

In fairness, Betty herself never claimed *Egg* was the gospel truth, or any of her other works for that matter. In fact she later argued that *Egg* was about 'an imaginary place in an imaginary country'. None of the disconnects with real life need alter the reader's enjoyment of the book. It can never truly be determined how much is fact and how much is fiction: Betty was writing for publication and quite rightly wanted to engage her readers. There may well have been editorial pressure; she originally wrote the book in journal form, for instance, but was asked to change it. What we do know for sure, because Betty used to tell stories about the farm to friends for years before she wrote the book, is that, just as in *Egg*, the farm had no electricity or indoor plumbing; the recalcitrant wood stove made heating the house and cooking meals a major undertaking; and when there was money for improvements Bob always insisted that the chickens got priority. Many of the elements in *The Egg and I* – the bats that fly in through the bedroom windows, the joys of going to the outhouse at night, the ice in the chicken houses, Betty's eccentric rural neighbors whom she enjoys because they are so different – were very much based in reality.

What also seem real are Betty's feelings and emotions, which make the book so much more than just a comic account of an inept farm wife. For her first year on the farm Betty writes that she feels constantly lonely, so much so that whenever she hears the sound of a car passing the end of the road she flings herself at the nearest window to see who it is. It's difficult to know what to make of Betty's repeated emphasis on her feelings of isolation, knowing that her mother and brother and sisters were all on a farm just a short distance down the road and that her other neighbors were much closer than the five miles she describes in *Egg*. But the frequent references to loneliness ring true. Perhaps Bob discouraged visits to her family, or perhaps Betty was simply unable to get away from their busy life and did indeed feel alone much of the time. There was no radio or telephone and she is likely to have been on her own for long periods, frequently in terrible weather which would have kept her indoors. There is so much mention of her loneliness in *Egg* that Betty's apparent feelings on this score carry real weight.

She was certainly alone in her marriage. Betty describes Bob as entirely impervious to the lowering gloom of the mountains and the solitary nature of their lives, and also pretty much indifferent to his wife's sensitivity. They appear to have nothing whatsoever in common. Betty reads voraciously and can't get enough books; Bob reads *American Poultryman*. Betty paints the local scenery in water-colors; Bob views artistic endeavor as some kind of intermittent medical aberration. She wrote that when the door closed on any departing guests, it closed also on any more dinner-time conversation between the two of them. And even this was not the whole story.

§

Books could have been an escape from loneliness but Betty can't get hold of any. Mary in later life maintained that, apart from abounding health and vitality, the Bards had three outstanding characteristics: an irresistible desire to help, a mania for talk, and an appetite for literature encompassing anything in print. Betty now has no-one to talk to and nothing to read. She loved reading with a passion but in *Egg* she has brought too few books, so has to read and re-read what little there is, plus any old newspapers, magazines and catalogs she can get her hands on. There is no hope of borrowing books from her mountain neighbors because they don't read; the mountain women pass the time 'embroidrying' all their clothes and bedlinen and handkerchiefs with hard scratchy knots, and consider reading to be boastful and lazy and an indication of general moral turpitude. Betty hates any form of embroidery and would rather be cross-stitched to death than take it up. She longs for more books but it's too difficult to get them sent from the city to such a lonely location. A ramshackle book shop in town only stocks titles like *Types of Manure and How to Know Them*, although the owner does send Betty some articles about a woman and her unemployed husband who by their own choice live in isolation on the Pacific Coast. The woman in question just *loves* all the privations, which like Betty's include no electricity, running water, or toilet. Betty suspects that Bob and the bookshop owner have colluded in sending the articles in order to point up her own defects, and she is so incensed by the woman's insane happiness with hardship that she throws the clippings across the room.

While the first spring and summer are bearable in the sunshine, fall and winter come as a crushing defeat to Betty's morale. It rains, and rains, and rains, and rains. The mountains, previously a glowering but passive presence, suddenly take to actively deluging the ranch with constant downpours. None of this can have come as a surprise, as Betty must already have experienced a Peninsula winter during her year on the family farm, but in *Egg* the winter deluges are painted as a new and depressing discovery. She is stuck in the little house all day and the smoky wood-burning stove is an increasingly sinister entity which refuses either to heat the house or cook the food unless coaxed with kerosene. In the summer and spring Betty hadn't cared how slow the stove was or how little heat it gave out. She and Bob were outdoors from dawn to dark, they allowed plenty of time for cooking things and all of the wood was dry. With the first rainy day she realizes that 'Stove' is her mortal enemy and would have to be handled with extreme caution. It appears to burn through all the fuel it's given while releasing no heat. They are cold all that first winter and surrounded by wet flapping washing which cannot be dried outside. Socks and underwear flap damply against Betty as she tries to cook, but she cannot take them down because they are essential items and need to be dried. After the strenuous spring and summer, she was looking forward to the winter as a time when she could curl up by a roaring fire and make rugs and quilts just like the farm people in all the books she had read. Obviously this is not to be as it takes her sixteen hours a day just to keep 'Stove' going and get the meals cooked, including dinner as their evening meal. Most of the mountain people eat their dinner at eleven in the morning and have their supper at five, but Betty clings to dinner at night as the last remnant of civilized life as taught by her elegant mother. There is no time for the winter neighborliness she had imagined, either, as all the usual chores take ten times as long in the cold and the dark and the wet. By January dusk is setting in at three in the afternoon, 'like a shroud'. On stormy days Betty lights the lamps early and stays close to the house and 'Stove'.

Sometimes Betty takes advantage of Bob's absence:

Some Saturday mornings, as soon as the mountains had bottled up the last cheerful sound of Bob and the truck, I, feeling like a cross between a boll weevil and a slut, took a large cup of hot coffee, a hot-water bottle, a cigarette and a magazine and WENT BACK TO BED. *Then, from six-thirty until nine or so, I luxuriated in breaking the old mountain tradition that a decent woman is in bed only between the hours of seven pm and four am unless she is in labor or dead.*

Along with the picture Betty paints of growing loneliness and gloom comes this hugely funny disenchantment with farming as a way of life. One of the most enjoyable aspects of *The Egg and I* is Betty's subversion of the rural idyll. Rugged pioneer women may have toiled heroically over their backbreaking tasks, eventually triumphing over adversity with a pristine farmhouse and abundant produce wrested from the land; Betty does not. For instance she is delighted, and doesn't mind saying so, when the pressure cooker explodes and she no longer has to face canning the mountains of fruit, vegetables, meat and fish hauled into the kitchen by an unfeeling Bob.

Day follows backbreaking day but at least Betty has her idiosyncratic neighbors to enjoy. First and foremost of these are the 'Kettles', a large and shiftless family subsisting on a ramshackle farm with much begging and borrowing off those nearby. Betty has a great deal of fun in *Egg* describing the mountainous, slatternly and foul-mouthed, if kindly, Maw (or Ma) Kettle, and the terminally lazy and feckless Paw who drives Bob insane with his countless requests for help with the plowing, the sowing, the haying, the milking, the barn cleaning, the chicken house building, the gardening, or the cess pool, while doing no work himself. The Kettles' kitchen has baby chicks behind the stove and cats with fleas, and their outhouse, in which Ma Kettle sits comfortably chatting to visitors, has no door. Their farm's failure to thrive is entirely due to Washington machinations and not at all to Paw's laziness or the dirt and animal malnutrition endemic on their homestead. Politicians are to blame for the fact that the manure is stacked so high in the barn that Paw can't get in to milk the cows, and as far as Maw is concerned the crooks in Washington can take their fancy laws and bribes and stuff 'em. Bob loathes the Kettles but Betty finds them comforting; their kitchen may be chaotic and somewhat heady, but it has a warm human feeling in comparison with Betty's own clean but lonely one. In their struggle for existence the Kettles have developed strong ties with each other; it's them against the world, and Betty appreciates being enfolded into their warmth.

Betty's actual neighbors, the Bishop family, certainly bore a striking resemblance to the fictional Kettles, if slightly fewer in number. Susanna Bishop seems to have been the model for Ma Kettle, although the Bishop family maintained that she never used swear words like Betty's character and was of very clean habits. Susanna's husband Albert Bishop was known in the neighborhood as a bit impractical, if not as downright inept and lazy as Pa Kettle, but like Pa he did once burn down a barn. The similarities were sufficient to cause Betty quite a bit of trouble after *The Egg and I* had been published. She had described Pa Kettle as having eyebrows growing together, a large red nose and a black derby hat; a photograph of the Bishops from 1946 shows Albert Bishop as both dark-browed and large-nosed. The Kettles' daughter 'Tits' in *The Egg and I* has young children just like the Bishops' real daughter Madeline around the time that Betty was living there. Madeline was called 'Toots' by her family (pronounced as in Tootsie Roll) and was married to a man who was half Native American and who developed problems with alcoholism; in the book 'Tits' has problems with her Native American husband who gets drunk on checks he receives from the government. There was more than enough cause for the Bishops to claim they were the originals for the Kettles when *The Egg and I* was published over fifteen years later.

Other local inhabitants pose more of a problem for Betty. In her book she makes no bones about fearing and disliking the Native Americans she comes across. These are likely to have been members or descendants of the S'Klallam tribe (the 'Strong People') or the now extinct Chimakum tribe, also known as the Port Townsend Native Americans, who lived on the Olympic Peninsula and after whom the Hesketts' local town of Chimacum was named. There may also have been members of the Quinault and Chinook tribes in the area. Native Americans had lived off the land of the Peninsula for thousands of years, making good use of the abundant natural resources – wild salmon from the rivers, and fish, seals and whales from the sea. They were known for their skill with canoes and superb knowledge of their surroundings, but their way of life had inevitably changed with the advent of European settlers. Successive waves of measles and smallpox epidemics wiped out whole villages. In the 1870s, settlers in the Washington Territory wanted land, and urged the Bureau of Indian Affairs to relocate all Native Americans to reservations, although after passage of the 1884 Indian Homestead Act several S'Klallam families did become landholders themselves. By establishing homesteads, however, the S'Klallam were compelled to end relations with other tribal members who did not, and many chose to leave their home areas altogether rather than do this. Those times were difficult for many because they had no permanent homes and their shanty villages were frequently dislocated by settler pressure. The S'Klallam also faced hunger due to trouble with fishing access: a 1910 Washington State law was passed that required a license, but the lack of US citizenship prevented tribal members from obtaining one. Even after 1924, when all Native Americans finally won citizenship, Washington State continued to limit its indigenous residents' right to fish.

Life was still difficult for the Native Americans when Betty was living on the Peninsula in 1927 but she is hardly sympathetic. As a very young child back in Butte, Betty had been attracted by the 'Indians'. Braves on ponies sometimes rode down Main Street followed by squaws on foot with papooses on their backs. These were the Blackfeet tribe, wearing beautifully beaded dresses and terrific feather headdresses. The children's grandmother Gammy had read them the stories of Hiawatha, Pocahontas and Sitting Bull, and had told them plenty of hair-raising tales of massacres, scalpings and running the gauntlet. As a result Betty and her siblings romantically viewed 'Indians' as wonderfully strong and brave and would run for blocks to see them. Now she was meeting them in person.

Her descriptions in *Egg* pull no punches. She dubs the Native Americans ignorant and dirty moonshine-drinkers, and worse. A number of the local 'Indians', called Geoduck (pronounced Gooeyduck), Clamface and Crowbar in *The Egg and I*, become buddies with Bob, but definitely not with Betty. She writes that they are excellent hunters and fishers and generous with what they catch, but that they knock their wives down for exercise and would never chop wood or carry water for them. They are unable to understand why manly Bob, a fine hunter and a crack shot, docilely fetches wood for Betty whenever asked instead of delivering a swift left to her chin and telling her to shut up. In the book Geoduck and a friend, both drunk, invade her kitchen when she is alone on the farm and very frightened; in her account she grabs a gun and manages to drive them off. (Bob just laughs when she tells him.) In another passage Betty attends a Native American beach picnic which she is horrified to find is an occasion for drinking to stupefaction. Babies crawl around neglected, women are shoved around and a young girl is molested by an older man. As a result of these experiences Betty is fearful and repulsed by the Native Americans she previously thought so wonderful, and is frank in saying so – seemingly failing to grasp, along with many others at that time, that the problems she describes stemmed from the damage done to their traditional way of life by white settlement.

But in Betty's account of the picnic she also describes speaking to an old tribeswoman who could remember when her people were warriors, and who had heard stories of a great war among the tribes in 1855. The old lady is the last of her tribe and seems troubled by the degeneration she now sees around her, Betty writes. The inclusion in *Egg* of this dialogue with the old woman is an indication that Betty nevertheless had an instinctive, if unconscious, sympathy with the Native American plight during her period on the Peninsula. In the end Betty does warm to some of the Native Americans, 'Geoduck' and the others among them, yet she remains frank about her dislike in general and some of her comments make troubling reading. But there was no such thing as political correctness in 1945 when she wrote the book, and Betty told it as she saw it: she was frightened by Bob's seemingly brutish friends, repelled by the drunkenness, and incensed by their attitude to women. Perhaps stark reality, with whatever cause, was too much of a contrast with her youthful imaginings about noble braves. However, Betty was no racist, and there would be plenty in her life and work to prove it.

Birth

Betty became pregnant either just before or just after her marriage to Bob in July 1927 and baby Anne was born in 1928, before the purchase of the farm. The pregnancy she describes in *Egg* was therefore her second, not her first, but in the book there is only ever mention of one child.

In *Egg* the mountain people call pregnancy being 'that way' and the news that young Betty Heskett is 'that way' soon gets around. One day when she and Bob are out in the car they are hailed by a complete stranger who climbs onto the car's running board and, his face uncomfortably close to Betty's, offers to fix her up for six dollars with a buttonhook. He has 'taken care of' someone else who was six months along and gotten rid of three for his own wife at three months. Betty, horrified, finds out at the doctor's office in town that the man's wife is in the hospital recovering from her latest abortion at her husband's hands. The girl in the office telling her this laughs heartily but Betty doesn't think it funny and asks why the man hasn't been stopped or arrested. If it isn't him it would be someone else, the girl tells her. Women would either find someone else to do it or produce an abortion themselves using buttonhooks or baling wire or hatpins. Abortion was still illegal at that point, but from Betty's account it appears that a number of poverty-stricken mountain women could not face the struggle of repeated pregnancy and child-rearing.

In *Egg* Betty's pregnancy isn't made any easier by Bob's insensitive discussion of worms, intestines and chicken lice at the breakfast table. She goes into labor just at the busiest time on the farm, according to her account in the book, and almost gives birth as Bob drives her at hair-raising speed into town. The baby pops out as soon as they reach the 'Town' hospital, after which she enjoys two weeks of heavenly rest.

This was St. John's Hospital in Port Townsend, at that time run by the Sisters of Providence, who raised their own chickens and vegetables and fed them to their lucky patients. In *Egg*, Betty describes how in the evenings the sisters sit sewing and talking and laughing in her room and how, with that kind of treatment, so very unlike her rough, hard-working existence on the farm, she is tempted to stay pregnant for the rest of her life.

Betty may well have glossed over the actual process of birth. Responding once to a comment that birth was just like a little case of indigestion, she joked that maybe so, but only if you'd swallowed a cement-mixer. Prior to the 1920s the majority of births in America had taken place at home, with little or no pain relief, and one of the biggest changes to American childbirth in that decade was the move from home to hospital. This at least offered women the opportunity of a lying-in period to recover, and the support of nurses to help care for the baby in the first few weeks. However, the 1920s was also characterized by a dramatic increase in childbirth interventions such as forceps, episiotomy and cesarean section. Fortunately there was also a greater choice in pain relief drugs. Ether and chloroform were widely used and many women were also given a combination of morphine and the drug scopolamine, which induced a sort of blackout called 'twilight sleep'. (Betty's sister Mary was to experience this during her own labors.) Betty later told Mary she was so thankful for a chance to lie down she didn't care what was happening. But whatever Betty's actual experience in having her child, her second daughter, Joan Dorothy Heskett, arrived healthy on 14 July 1929 at St. John's. Joan's big sister, Anne Elizabeth Heskett, had been born the year before in Seattle General Hospital, just as healthy – and red-haired, in the good old Bard tradition.

In *Egg* life is twice as hard on the farm with a new baby, and when she gets back Betty has to really run to keep up with the work, which now includes looking after hundreds of baby chicks as well as her own newborn. Betty's life becomes a living nightmare – starting at four in the morning – of household tasks interspersed with running out to attend to the chicks. This goes on and on throughout the day. It felt like fleeing down the track just ahead of a rushing locomotive bearing down on her, she wrote. Her chicken manual warns that a single drink of cold water could be fatal for a chick and Betty looks longingly at their icy little lake. Other farm animals have also been busy producing and along with her own baby and the chicks, all of the other small, screaming, voracious young are assigned to her care. Feeding them, herself, Bob and the baby becomes Betty's perpetual task.

Bob's life is just as hard as hers, clearing land, pulling tree stumps or unrolling wire. Their conversation becomes limited to grunts at mealtimes as they hurry their food and flick through seed catalogs. There is little time for romance and when Bob one night unexpectedly kisses the back of her neck, Betty is as confused as if a boss had rewarded her in this way for her typing.

Life continued. In *Egg* Betty cooks, washes, looks after the baby (in real life, two babies), grows vegetables, helps Bob and, as ever, cares for the chickens and cleans out the chicken houses. On and on goes the monotonous work of feeding and watering, conducting post-mortems on dead chickens, keeping detailed egg records, dressing cockerels for market, helping Bob with the culling, and gathering pullets from the tops of trees at night to put them to roost in the chicken houses out of the way of predators.

But it isn't all chickens and loneliness. In *Egg* there is the occasional Saturday night dance, often many miles away; movies in nearby or not so nearby towns, where Betty loses all interest in the plot if the heroine has modern conveniences and takes long steamy baths; county fairs, which Betty enjoys, if saddened by the loneliness implicit in the many fancywork exhibits on display; and occasional private events such as the 'Indian' beach picnic or the famous occasion of Mrs Kettle's birthday, when the men drink on the back porch and talk non-stop about sex while the women cook in the kitchen and talk non-stop about sex. There is the excitement, and horror, of the occasional cougar or bear lurking around the farm. Things get easier when Bob installs water pipes and at last there is running water in the kitchen. Through it all, though, runs the slowly unraveling thread, faint but discernible, of the disintegration of Bob and Betty's marriage.

By 1930, after about three years on the farm, Betty had had enough. Not just of the chickens, which in *Egg* she now hates with a vengeance, especially the chicks. She writes that the dear fluffy little babies are stupid, smell, peck each other's eyes out, require constant feeding and watering and are hell-bent on killing themselves by drowning in the water fountains or coming down with diseases. She also can't take the isolation and the rain in the winter months a minute longer. The hard work of the farm is easier and more enjoyable in the spring and summer (despite the canning) but she has been broken by the other seasons: waking up in the mornings to the persistent battering of rain on the roof and then going to bed to the same sound, knowing that there was nothing ahead but more rain and wind and loneliness.

But most importantly, her relationship with Bob has disintegrated. *The Egg and I* ends with Betty and Bob thinking about buying a new chicken ranch with a nice modern farmhouse. The reality was that Betty was suddenly impelled to take flight, taking the children with her. In *Anybody Can Do Anything* she describes her flight as due to this combination of too many chickens, the depressing winters and the increasing alienation from Bob, from whom she is now poles apart emotionally. She reflects in *Egg* that Bob is more interested in how much weight her shoulder can carry, than with the shoulder itself. She muses that she has obediently followed her mother's well-meant advice in falling in with her husband's plans in order to keep him happy, and trying to learn to like chicken farming on a lonely ranch. Now she wonders if there is something wrong with her, as only Bob turned out to be happy. Instead of enjoying living in the wilderness she feels she is pitting herself against mountains and millions of trees and failing dismally. Perhaps Sydney had the pioneer spirit for it, she says to herself; she has not.

There was, of course, much more to the failure of the marriage than these musings for public consumption. In her subsequent divorce submission Betty claimed that Bob had been a brutal and abusive husband during the whole of their married life; she had clearly had experiences on the farm that never made it into *The Egg and I*.

The 1931 application to the Superior Court of the State of Washington for King County stated that Bob failed to do his part on the farm and left everything to Betty. The greater part of raising the chickens had fallen to Betty's lot, and the living and returns from this labor were very meager. She had been obliged to work 'beyond her strength' in carrying water and gathering wood to keep herself and the babies from cold (an accusation confirmed by Betty's neighbor Bud, grandson of the Bishops, who later in life talked of the wood he used to cut for Betty and the little girls to keep them from freezing). Bob had neglected and refused to make provision for his family, now and during the marriage, the application charged. He was an alcoholic and was frequently drunken and abusive. On one occasion, according to the statement, he had poured coal oil on the side of the house and set it on fire, and it was only through a timely discovery by Betty and her younger sister (probably Dede) that destruction of the house and injury to the family were averted. (Some sources suggest that Bob was running a moonshine operation, and Betty in letters to her agent and publisher did discuss the need to remove references to illegal alcohol. There is still frequent mention of moonshine in

Egg, however, including Bob drinking it with his Native American friends.)

Betty's divorce application also claimed physical abuse. Bob had been guilty of cruel treatment and of heaping 'personal indignities' upon her, Betty claimed. He had 'struck and kicked plaintiff on a number of occasions', including when she was heavily pregnant with her first child, and had threatened to shoot both her and the children. He had called Betty vile names, and threatened to disfigure her so that no-one would ever care for her again.

This list of Bob's misdemeanors was 'greatly abbreviated', Betty stated later in the divorce process. For her part, Betty claimed to have done her utmost to make the marriage work. There had been many promises from Bob to do better and because of these promises Betty had stayed in the marriage, but her life had been miserable and unhappy from the very start. She had lost all affection for Bob and it would be impossible for her ever to live with him again.

Privately, Betty told her old friend Blanche that Bob had no sense of humor, hung around with crummy friends, and dramatized himself too much. She said that her grandmother had helped them buy a new car but that Bob had wrecked it the first day they owned it, and since the accident was his fault they were unable to collect any insurance. She told Blanche how she and Bob had once been invited to a party by one of his undesirable friends. Betty refused to go, but Bob, even though he knew how she felt about these particular people, nevertheless insisted. His method of persuasion was to pour a cup of kerosene onto the back porch and then hold a lighted match about ten inches above and threaten to drop it (seemingly the same or a similar incident to that related in the divorce application). Knowing Bob, Betty told Blanche she thought she had better agree to go to the party. Laughing, she said she'd had a terrible time there. Betty never acted the martyr.

Bob seems to have made Betty's life more of a hell on earth than the amusing rural existence she later conjured up in *Egg*. Given all this it's surprising how generous Betty is to Bob in the book. She praises his scientific chicken farming, carpentry, and marksmanship skills, more than once. The worst she delivers is calling him repellently cheerful, and callously impervious to the loneliness she herself felt. No doubt Betty had some knowledge of his inner demons. It seems likely that whatever happened during his period in the military may have caused some damage to the young soldier. Bob left the US Marines with Post Traumatic Stress Disorder and there are reports that he suffered with night terrors; perhaps Betty was being as forgiving as she could be, and Bob was after all the father of her children, who by the time she wrote *Egg* were old enough to read and understand the book.

In *Anybody Can Do Anything* Betty describes her flight from the farm as a lonely, rain-sodden walk through dripping brush as she leads three-year-old Anne by one hand and carries both a suitcase and year-and-a-half-old Joan in the other. Thus encumbered, and entirely on her own, she takes a bus, a ferry and another bus to reach Seattle.

The reality of Betty's escape may have been rather different. According to Blanche's memoir, Mary went to the farm to rescue her sister and told Blanche that she had made the rescue trip to Chimacum when she knew Bob would not be there. She helped Betty pack her things and those of the girls and they left hurriedly, leaving no word behind. Whatever the precise circumstances of Betty's flight, she went, taking the girls with her and then filing for the divorce on grounds of cruelty. The only other alternatives at that time were adultery or desertion.

Divorce was granted in 1935 and Betty was awarded custody of the children. After the divorce, contact between the ex-spouses was virtually non-existent. Anne and Joan never saw their father again.

Betty and the Great Depression

AFTER THEIR FLIGHT from the farm Betty and the little girls moved in with her mother Sydney, brother Cleve, and sisters Mary, Alison and Dede, who were now all living in their new home close to Seattle's University District. The area got its name, not surprisingly, from the presence there of the University of Washington campus. Then as now the university set the tone for the neighborhood, with its famous University Bookstore, crowds of students and lively fraternity and sorority houses. Noisy streetcars clattered up University Way, still known as the 'Ave' from when it used to be 14th Avenue; young people in cars cruised up and down, occasionally stopping at one of the inexpensive coffee shops catering to impecunious students. The arts were flourishing: throughout the 1930s the Repertory Playhouse in its refurbished brick storehouse at 41st and University Way attracted large audiences with productions of the classics.

The Bards' modest house at 6317 15th Avenue NE had been built in 1910, when local property development had burgeoned following the previous year's Alaska-Yukon-Pacific Exposition held on the university campus. Initially part of the University District, the neighborhood gradually assumed the title of the Roosevelt District after the opening of Betty's old school, Roosevelt High, in 1922. Number 6317, just north of Cowen Park, was a four-bedroom family home with a shingled roof. Sydney had bought the house in Dede and Alison's names, listing herself as guardian, which suggests that she used the girls' share of the money from the Montana mine. She eventually took out a second mortgage on the property, and then a third and even a fourth.

Courtesy Puget Sound Regional Archives

Outside, the streetcar line ran directly past the house. Inside, the already large family somehow made room for Betty and the children, and never had home been more welcoming.

> *It's a wonderful thing to know that you can come home any time from anywhere and just open the door and belong. That everybody will shift until you fit and that from that day on it's a matter of sharing everything...when you share unhappiness, loneliness, and anxiety about the future with a mother, a brother, and three sisters, there isn't much left for you. (Anybody Can Do Anything)*

After their isolated existence little Anne and Joan were excited by the unexpected chaos and laughter of a large household, and it was exhilarating for Betty to be home after her experiences on the farm and her troubles with Bob. She and the girls could stare in wonder at the large department stores downtown, the Bon Marché at Third and Pine and the more upscale Frederick & Nelson, two blocks away, where the famous chocolate Frango mints were newly on sale; or the store on Second Avenue recently opened by two brothers who had given it their own last name of Nordstrom. In the toy departments that Christmas, Betty could have bought the girls the latest in playthings, the Fisher-Price duck on a string which quacked when pulled, or a Raggedy Ann doll. The world had changed since Betty had been away. She wrote that on her return she was amazed by the city's dazzling new multicolored neon lights, swooping as they spelled out the names of shops and restaurants. In New York the Empire State Building, the world's tallest skyscraper, had just been completed. A new era had begun.

But, at the age of twenty-three, Betty was a single parent and jobless. She needed to support herself and her tiny daughters and it was the worst possible time to be looking for a job. The Depression was beginning to bite. The Wall Street crash of 1929 had undermined business investment and consumer confidence, and there had been a sharp economic decline. Initially the residents of Washington State, so far from Wall Street, had failed to react to these reverses. Even as the stock market plummeted the *Seattle Times* declared 'No Depression', and indeed for the first year job losses were minimal. But hopes faded towards the end of the following year as the banks began to fail, stores everywhere put up their shutters and unemployment escalated. By late 1931 wages in America had fallen by about a third and in Seattle as many as 20,000 were out of work. Shipping and shipbuilding in the area had ground to a halt, forty Northwest lumber mills had closed, and a few blocks south of the city's Pioneer Square hundreds of unemployed men lived in a shantytown known ironically as 'Hooverville', after President Herbert Hoover's ineffective relief policies. There was no unemployment insurance and lost work quickly translated into lost homes and extreme poverty. Soup kitchens and breadlines were serving ever greater numbers of people, the tattered men and women lining up for hours before the doors opened. In the midst of this desperation Betty now had to find a job. She knew very quickly that she wasn't going to be able to rely on any financial support from Bob, whose name she now dropped, reverting to Bard.

By Betty's own admission she had no marketable skills. She did have one thing on her side, though: the redoubtable red-haired Mary, who in Betty's famous phrase believed that anybody could do anything, especially Betty. Mary, of course, had plenty of confidence. In *Anybody Can Do Anything*, Betty's book about trying to earn a living in the Depression, Mary breezes into offices and manages to secure jobs or orders for advertising by taking a close personal interest in the life and loves of everyone in the company and cheering them up with total lies. She makes friends all over Seattle, is a favorite client at the employment agencies, and never has any trouble getting new jobs. Mary buoys Betty up, telling her that the world is crawling with cowed employees, 'white-faced creeps' who can take down someone else's ideas at two hundred words a minute, but that the Bards have ideas of their own and should use their brains. Naturally, Mary's ideas about Betty's talents don't match Betty's far more modest estimation: she feels she's fit only for a very undemanding job involving filing, slow typing and keeping the office clean.

Despite these misgivings Betty starts to feel that life is suddenly full of promise and that soon she, too, will be one of the morning commuters swaying on the streetcar on her way to a wonderful new job. The only problem is that, after her lonely sojourn in the mountains rearing chickens and never seeing anybody, Betty is severely lacking in self-confidence. Starting at the first of the many jobs Mary arranges for her she describes herself at this point as very thin, and pale with fright. In *Anybody*, with her then long red hair parted in the middle and pulled tightly back into a knot, she feels she looks like one of those white-faced creeps Mary is always talking about. She also feels she has little to offer prospective employers. She can't do shorthand and goes to pieces the moment an employer asks her to take a letter; unable to read her own hieroglyphics, she brings them home at night for Mary to decipher. She can't type more than twenty words a minute. She strives to look efficient because she is so afraid of being fired and pretends to know how a filing system works because she is too diffident to admit she doesn't, and then makes howling errors as she haphazardly files documents which can never be found again. When first working as a secretary she makes terrible mistakes, using up reams of paper and leaving little holes in her typed letters from deeply gouged erasures. Scared and anxious, she is simply unable to apply some of her undoubtedly sharp intelligence to the various problems which confront her. Over time she does get better, although never ceasing to find office work dull.

In *Anybody* Mary first gets Betty jobs working as secretary to a mining engineer and to a lumberman. Eventually Betty works for a rabbit-grower, a lawyer, a credit bureau, a florist, a public stenographer, a dentist, a laboratory of clinical medicine, a gangster, and a pyramid scheme. She also hand-tints photographs and sells advertising (badly). Maybe these jobs don't last, but she is rarely out of work, mostly thanks to Mary. These many and varied jobs were to provide a rich seam of comic material for *Anybody Can Do Anything*.

§

Soon after her return to Seattle Betty filed for divorce from Bob, the first step in what was to be a long-drawn-out process. In fact she filed for divorce twice, initially in June 1930 with the help of her friend Margaret Bundy's father Edward as attorney, and then again a year later. On the occasion of the first application, at which point Betty was staying with Mary in her Seattle apartment, the judge ordered Bob to appear in court and not to dispose of any of the farm or the flock of seven hundred chickens. The property had been secured with the help of Betty's share of the Bards' Montana mine windfall and therefore belonged to Betty alone. But, either ignoring the order or receiving it too late, Bob went ahead and sold both the flock and some of their household effects. Astonishingly, he is recorded as passing nearly all of the resultant sum, $450, to Betty's attorney, acknowledging her sole ownership of the property and also deeding her a sum in equity. Soon afterwards he left Chimacum, and at some point during the following year he and Betty returned to the ranch to pick up her books and wedding presents. They found other people living in the house and using their things. Some of their belongings were never found at all.

The outcome of the first filing for divorce is not clear, but as Betty's second filing in 1931 referred to Bob's promises to do better, and showed that Betty had continued to live with him, it appears that a reconciliation was attempted. It failed.

On her own again, Betty desperately needed money. Some of the Montana mine funds had also gone into maintenance of the farm and support for the family, including hospital bills for both Bob and herself. Of these funds nothing now remained. In *Egg* Betty describes buying the farm for cash but in fact it had been bought on a real-estate contract for $560, of which more than $450 was still owing. However, the equity that Bob deeded to Betty was only $50, and according to Betty's divorce filing he had only contributed about $300 of his own money during their entire time on the farm. The sale of the farm would bring her nothing. There were other debts, too: $55 in hospital bills still owing for Anne's birth and $35 for Joan's, to doctors in Seattle and Port Townsend. Betty was also personally liable for other bills and, according to her 1931 divorce application, had been threatened with legal action.

Betty's attorney requested divorce and custody of the children, subject to visitation; that Bob pay in installments a sum of $1500 into a suitable saving fund for Anne and Joan's education; that he repay Betty for the wrongful removal from the ranch of Betty's longed-for water system and tank, the money from which he had kept for his own use; that he pay all outstanding bills and that his employer, the insurance company to which he had returned after leaving the farm, be restrained from any further payments to him pending further orders of the court. The attorney also requested that Bob pay $150 per month for the care, support and education of the girls, that he pay the costs of the divorce, and that Betty be allowed further financial relief from him as required. According to the attorney Betty was unskilled and unable to earn sufficient for the care of herself and her two daughters and was currently having to rely on the charity of her family. He asked for temporary alimony of $40 a week and the sum of $75 towards the cost of her suit.

In July 1931 there was a response from Bob's lawyers. In an affidavit Bob claimed that he had always attempted to provide for his family to the best of his ability, and that he had no funds or property to meet his expenses beyond about $50 pocket money. He was having to borrow money to live until his sales commissions became due and payable by his company. It was his belief that Betty was now gainfully employed at a lumber company in Seattle, earning $100 a month and living with her family, and was therefore well provided for.

Battle had commenced. Betty for her part responded through her attorney that she was earning less than $100 a month and had to attend night school, at a cost to her for meals downtown and incidentals in connection with the course, of about $15 a month. Her father was dead and her mother a widow without means of support, her statement continued, and the seven members of her mother's household – her mother, her two younger sisters, her elder sister Mary, herself and the children (no mention of Cleve) – were totally dependent on Betty and her sister Mary's earnings. It would be impossible for her to support herself and her daughters without help.

Bob's employers, the Mutual Life Insurance Company, had meanwhile denied that any money was due to him and had sworn on oath that in fact he owed *them* money. On 27 July the court ordered Bob to pay Betty $20 a month. Up until this bad news from his employer, Betty had been under the impression that Bob was earning about $400 a month and had a sum of $900 coming to him, as prior to the break-up he had deliberately misled her by showing her old sales slips for thousands of dollars' worth of insurance which he claimed to be getting commission on at renewal.

Bob's next move was to demand custody of Anne and Joan – probably just a feint to frighten Betty – and to claim that he had only quit the insurance business to go into chicken farming at the 'express insistence and desire' of Betty and her mother and brother. He did admit that Betty had worked very hard to make the business succeed. Betty argued back that Bob was not a fit and proper person to have charge of the children, and absolutely denied the claims that he had been pressured into the chicken business by her family. The $20 a month in support ordered by the court was not paid and Bob was duly threatened with a contempt of court charge possibly leading to prison. And so it went on.

§

There was to be little support from Bob and even with fairly regular, if temporary, work, the reality of being a single parent with two small children to feed during the Depression was no joke. Food was often short in the Bard household, and even fuel. Mary was sued by the Pacific Coast Coal Company for failure to pay, and a lien was once placed on the Bards' home by an unpaid workman. The family kept their lights turned off much of the time and one winter even had to burn books in their furnace to keep warm. In *Anybody*, Mary successfully threatens to sue the president of the telephone company when they are about to disconnect the family's telephone and then tries the same thing with the power and light company, but the electricity is disconnected anyway and the family is left burning old Christmas candles to light the house. When they run out of firewood, Mary unearths an old bucksaw and marches them all down to the city park to saw up fallen logs. Two park gardeners come up and ask them what they think they are doing, so Mary tells them, and to the family's surprise and relief the gardeners offer to help them with the sawing and to carry the wood back to the house. Thereafter the gardeners save the logs and bark for them.

The family can't afford entertainment and so read books rather than going to the movies and play Chinese checkers instead of going to concerts. With so little money and with so many females in the family the older Bard women all wear each other's clothes (the first one up was the best dressed, Betty wrote), and also have to endure teenage Alison and her high-school friends wearing their clothes behind their backs so that nothing they own ever really cools down. The Bard categories for clothes are 'clean', 'dirty', 'work', 'date' and 'terrible', which is for wearing around the house. Mary is clever and courageous enough to alter old clothes for herself and come up with something wonderful by grafting the bodice of one old dress onto the skirt of another, but Betty doesn't have the talent.

Buying something new was not an option. A Frederick & Nelson lingerie advertisement in 1932 offered lacy crepe slips at $2.95 and satin and lace panties at $1.95. ('It isn't the cost that counts – look what a lot of loveliness you can buy here for very little money.') Dresses were available from $10, and hosiery cost 75c. But at that time a stenographer's monthly wages could be as low as $50. With food prices having risen 30% in the early years of the Depression, and with two small children to feed and clothe, Betty would simply not have had the money to buy new.

Shoes are another problem in *Anybody*. Anne and Joan keep growing out of theirs and must have proper replacements, but for themselves the adults in the family buy cheap imitations of good brands which generally work as long as they can stand the pain and don't go out in the rain. There's a little shoemaker in the neighborhood who works wonders with his repairs for just a few cents, and Mary and Betty wait at home in their stockinged feet while one of the younger ones runs up to the store with shoes in hand.

15th Avenue in 1934
Seattle Municipal Archives, licensed under CC by 2.0

The struggle with Bob continued. He paid nothing to Betty in December 1931 and January 1932 and was ordered to appear before the judge. Betty requested that the temporary alimony and support money he was supposed to be paying be raised to $50 a month. The $20 a month she was meant to be getting, but wasn't, was not enough. In February she had the unpleasant experience of being in court with Bob in an attempt to recover the money; Bob promised to pay the $40 he owed but failed to do so, even though he had been earning $100 a month in commissions since June the previous year. By 24 February he had been ordered to pay the $60 now due or be committed to the King County Stockade for contempt of court. He was arrested, but found to be 'temporarily incapacitated' by a physical injury, and given till March to pay. Finally, in March, the money appeared.

Both parties were in court again in April when it was decreed that after the expiration of six months Betty was entitled to a full divorce on the grounds she had presented. She was given custody of the children, subject to reasonable visitation at times of her choosing, and Bob was to pay $30 support each month plus the costs of Betty's attorney, the costs of the action, and the judgment fee.

Betty, meanwhile, was left for the most part without financial support. Her old school friend Blanche sometimes visited Sydney when the rest of the family were out and could see that the Bards were suffering. Sydney would be baking or gardening or sitting in a corner of the sofa with a coffee on the table in front of her, a tome from Galsworthy's *Forsyte Saga* or an Angela Thirkell novel in one hand and a Camel cigarette in the other (all the older Bards continued smoking during the Depression, even though they sometimes had to flip a quarter to decide whether to buy bread or cigarettes). A couple of dogs would be at her feet. As warm and welcoming as ever, Sydney invariably made Blanche feel as though she had been sitting there just waiting for her to come by. During these visits it was evident to Blanche that the Bards were feeling the pinch: the furniture was getting old and the carpeting a bit threadbare. Only Mary and Betty were working and every so often Betty would have to go to court to get the support money that Bob was supposed to be providing. This and Mary and Betty's pay was the only income for the whole family, and it was pooled and distributed to the best of Mary, Betty and Sydney's ability but it was a losing battle. Betty wrote in *Anybody* that it was like climbing a hill: they would just be getting to the top when something would break, or need replacing, or Christmas would come, and down they would plummet again. She and Mary essentially carried the household, with Mary naturally taking the lead. Family friend Margaret Bundy recalled that Mary's decisiveness, about matters fiscal as well as everything else, never failed, although it led her into all sorts of complications. Margaret could see both the positives and the negatives about Mary: fundamentally honest, yet with streaks of deception; conventional and yet scoffing at convention; aware of the imbecilities of the social world and yet taken in by them; warm and giving but at times 'coldly selfish and cruel'.

Mary, of course, was still inviting everybody she felt sorry for to stay for dinner or all night or even to move in. Dinner would only be cheap dishes which could be stretched, like barley and oxtails or meatloaf, and Blanche remembered that sometimes it was even just lima beans or rice. Sydney would season the food well, bring it in on her lovely marigold Wedgwood platters, and serve it using her ornate serving set. According to Blanche an elegant dinner party atmosphere prevailed and Sydney, who sometimes cooked in the fireplace when the electricity had been cut off, never apologized for the menu.

In *Anybody*, Mary and Betty make their own sandwiches for lunch at work and often eat them in the upstairs dining-room at Seattle's Pike Place Market, where they can enjoy the spectacular view of the waterfront. Mary and their mutual friends carry their sandwiches boldly in paper bags; others, less audacious, slip their food out of their briefcases or pockets as furtively as if they are smuggling drugs. Betty too is ashamed, especially when it's Mary's turn to make the sandwiches. She slaps them together and then stuffs them into anything that comes to hand – old bread wrapping and even newspaper and string. Mary, born with absolutely no false pride, merely laughs at Betty's sensitivity.

Blanche in her memoir remembered a young man coming to the Bards' door one day while she was visiting. Sydney welcomed him in for coffee, asking about his new baby and if he had finished painting the baby's room. Blanche assumed they were old friends but after two cups of coffee and several cigarettes, the young man tentatively asked for payment for the wood he'd delivered to Sydney a couple of weeks ago. Sydney answered kindly that she hadn't a cent in the house but that if he dropped back in the evening she would get the money off Mary, who was getting paid that day.

The young man is likely to have been one of Sydney's large collection of 'at the doors', itinerant and often desperate people running small businesses door to door as described by Betty in *Anybody Can Do Anything*. Sydney can't be persuaded to drop any because she feels so sorry for them. Mary and Betty didn't forget those worse off than themselves either; in 1932 they were both manning booths at a Red Cross drive. However, Sydney's hopelessness with money – presented in *Anybody* as a charming peccadillo – in fact drove Mary and Betty to distraction. Betty once observed that when she was young, if she had asked her mother for sixty dollars for stockings and there was only sixty dollars in the house, her mother would have given it to her.

Blanche recalled also that Betty and Mary had once gone to the bank to see about procuring a mortgage on the house. The two were shown in to see the vice-president, who was very stiff in a three-piece suit, thick glasses and highly polished shoes. Telling the story to Blanche, Betty had confessed to feeling a little overwhelmed when shown into the plush office with its heavy green carpets and green leather chairs studded with shiny brass upholstery tacks. Even bold Mary was uncomfortable and nervous in this august presence, and when the banker touched upon the subject of collateral she suddenly interrupted him and said facetiously, 'All we have are our two white bodies to offer for that.' The banker coughed a dry cough, bit his lower lip, and forced a weak little smile. Betty did not reveal whether they got the mortgage, and Blanche deemed this the essence of the Bards: they flung convention to the winds and made finance, even in those hard times, seem mundane and secondary to getting some fun out of life.

They certainly did have fun (at least in retrospect), despite the sad state of their finances. During the 1930s Mary became involved with the Seattle Repertory Playhouse run by Florence and Burton James, who were producing plays in their converted old storehouse in the University District. She, and Betty, may first have met the Jameses at the Cornish School they attended as young girls when Florence and Burton were heading the drama department there. The Bards seemed to have known the Jameses well, as Florence accompanied Betty and Blanche on a trip to nearby Victoria, British Columbia, some time around 1936. The Bard household would often play host to impromptu cast parties and there are hints that Mary herself may have acted, although her name does not appear on cast lists.

The 1930s was in fact a period of intense artistic experimentation and creativity. The social unrest of the Depression heightened political content, and government funding paid for artists in many spheres to be employed in an array of projects designed to create jobs. The leaders of such projects were often interested in nurturing regional talent and national culture. In Washington State the Depression became an exciting period for the arts, if not for other aspects of life, and Mary made the most of it. Home became a place where Betty met Mary's acting friends from the Playhouse and many others from Mary's artistic circle: painters, writers and musicians. With all these males milling about, Mary began to take her sister's love life in hand as well as her business career. In *Anybody* she finds dates for Betty, or at least uses her as a try-out for her own dates. Betty, of course, although the mother of two children, was still only in her twenties.

Soon after Betty's return from the farm Mary invited Betty and Blanche along on a date with someone who claimed to be a German baron. Betty and Blanche were to bring their own dates so that Mary could feel safer with the baron, who was what the family called a *body-thinko,* the Bard term for someone oversexed or who talked excessively about his ailments. Other Bardisms were a *smell-badall* for an obnoxious person of either sex; a *saddo* for someone consumed with self-pity; a *get-in-good-with-the-company* for a toady; and a *my-husband-saider* for a woman who quoted her husband constantly and had few ideas of her own. A *pee-pee talker* used barnyard talk and four-letter words, and a *be-happy* was a person not sincerely happy but merely pretending to be. Sydney had no time for people who told off-color jokes or used vulgar words. The family also preferred the scientific name for parts of the body.

Blanche's date was initially reluctant to go along on the outing with the baron because he said the Bards were all screwy, but was eventually persuaded. Mary decided they should all have new dresses and picked up some material from a friend's wholesale outlet. Blanche thought at first that it was awning material: black-and-white stripes, two inches wide, for Mary, yellow-and-white stripes of the same width for Betty, which Mary said would go perfectly with Betty's reddish-brown hair, and blue-and-white stripes for Blanche with her blue eyes. The pattern was simple: strapless, with a tight bodice and long, billowy skirt. Blanche, smaller than the other two, wondered if two-inch stripes would be right for her but as usual both she and Betty went along with anything Mary suggested.

The sewing-machine hummed all afternoon and well into the night. As they tried the dresses on in the living room the next day, other members of the family would occasionally walk through. Betty's brother Cleve did a double-take.

'My God, where's the circus? Sydney, I wouldn't let them out of the house in those tents.'

Mary riposted that stripes were very much the mode and Sydney, ever the peace-maker, told the girls they all looked charming and unique and that she was sure the baron had never dated German girls dressed quite so strikingly.

When the special evening finally came, Sydney sat in her favorite spot at the end of the sofa, her dogs at her feet. The three girls were grouped together like zebras waiting for their prey, as Blanche described it. Mary answered the knock at the door.

'Ah, the baron!' she greeted him, dramatically. The self-styled baron presented Mary with a floral box.

'An orchid,' she screamed, 'and yellow – my favorite!'

Running over to Sydney she asked her mother to pin it on her. Against the black-and-white stripes it gave the effect of an orchid peeking through an iron fence, Blanche recalled, but Mary's enthusiasm for the occasion trumped any incongruity. Sydney, after pinning the orchid in place, sat silently, smoking her cigarette with a smile on her face. She was highly amused.

After introductions to Betty and Blanche and their dates, the group headed for Willard's Roadhouse. By 1930 most people owned cars, and more roadhouses had sprung up along the main highways. The buildings were attractive by night but usually a little tacky-looking by day, Blanche remembered. The atmosphere inside Willard's was seductive, with little rose-shaded electric lamps that simulated candlelight on all the tables and window sills. The orchestra was playing a fox-trot as the party was ushered into a private room reserved by the baron, and seated at a round table for six. They ordered chicken and steak dinners with French fries and peas, and despite Prohibition there was plenty of liquor to go with it. Betty enjoyed herself because this was her first big night out since she had returned to Seattle from the chicken ranch, although, still licking her wounds from her broken marriage, she was reserved with her date. This was Jock Hutchings, an old boyfriend of Mary's.

When Mary returned from a dance with Blanche's partner she joked that he'd been trying to do the 'rape gavotte' with her. Blanche was taken aback, just as she had been when Mary announced she had been kissed back in the days of their girlhood. Most of her contemporaries hardly knew what the word 'rape' meant, and in those days if you did know the word you whispered it behind your hand. But Mary was always so open about everything and so uniquely funny Blanche never thought of being shocked, only amused.

Blanche eventually became engaged to Mary's former boyfriend Jock and the Bard sisters made some of the food for her engagement party. Betty and Mary turned white sandwich bread, green peppers, asparagus spears, shrimp, cucumbers and stuffed olives into works of art. A week before the event, Mary again took Betty and Blanche to pick out dresses at a wholesale house. Mary chose soft green, Betty, yellow, and Blanche, blue. The dresses were made of filmy chiffon with scoop necks, big three-quarter sleeves, and flowing long skirts with attached slips underneath. At the party Betty sat back as she quietly sized up people and situations to be hashed over later and enjoyed again, while Mary with her usual vivacity kept the event going with funny remarks. When Mary had been dating Jock herself she had not got on well with Jock's overbearing mother, but at the party the two were perfectly friendly. The ever observant Betty quietly commented that it was because Mary no longer posed a threat.

To thank the girls Blanche went to the Bards' the next day with perfume, and Sydney told Blanche she wanted to give her a wedding gift. She knew that Blanche had often admired her Wedgwood platters, one of which was at that point on the floor for the dog. Times being what they were and unable to afford to buy anything, Sydney reached down to the floor, picked up the platter, and went to the sink to run hot water over it.

'I hope you don't mind the dog's having used it; he just finished the left-over meatloaf,' she said.

Blanche loved the way Sydney treated her dogs as just another member of the family, and as far as she was concerned this was the perfect way to be presented with a wedding gift.

Mary

Then it was Mary's turn to get married. In *Anybody* Betty commented that Mary had been serially engaged, first to a Christian Scientist, then to a Jewish boy, and then to an actor. Now she had fallen properly for a doctor called Clyde Jensen. It was through Betty that they met. Mary, very ill with a chest infection, was struggling to cope with her busy radio promotion job at an advertising agency; Betty was working for an insurance company and therefore a self-declared authority on physical examinations. She insisted that Mary have a complete physical. Sydney phoned the hospital and was given Dr. Jensen's name, and the rest was history. Mary told Blanche that she had enticed her intended by allowing her wonderful curly auburn hair to lose its pins and fall flowingly down her back as they sat in a field of purple lupines after a picnic; her plan was for Clyde to find the color of her hair against the flowers irresistible, and clearly she succeeded. The *Seattle Times* in May 1934 reported the engagement of Miss Mary Ten Eyck Bard to Dr. Clyde Reynolds Jensen, describing Mary as a graduate of St. Nicholas School (somewhat overstating the case, as in fact Mary had been switched to a public school after Darsie's death) and as 'one of the city's prominent advertising women'. According to the report Mary had also been on the acting staff of the Seattle Repertory Playhouse. Blanche remembered that when Mary's friends threw parties for her engagement they didn't bother organizing any party games but simply relied on Betty to keep people amused with her witty stories about life on the chicken ranch.

Mary and Clyde were married early in the morning on 1 July 1934 in a chapel in St. Mark's Cathedral. Mary, who was twenty-nine, was given away by her brother Cleve. She wore a sand-beige dress and a cape trimmed with sand-colored Russian wolf, and carried a bouquet of Talisman roses. Betty as matron-of-honor wore a linen suit with brown lapels and a brown hat, and carried yellow roses; Sydney was in a dark blue and white print dress with dark blue accessories. Anne and Joan were bridesmaids in matching red English lawn dresses and carried red and blue garden bouquets. The early ceremony was necessary in order to catch a boat to the city of Victoria in Canada (the same location as Betty's honeymoon with Bob) and then on to the north end of Vancouver Island; immediately thereafter Mary became a busy doctor's wife and, eventually, the mother of three daughters.

*Courtesy Junior League of Seattle,
Puget Soundings*

Mary too became a writer, and in her 1949 book *The Doctor Wears Three Faces* she describes a visit to Sydney and the family after Clyde has been operated on for appendicitis. She and Betty spend the afternoon in the shops before retreating to the love and comfort of home:

> ...we spent the afternoon trying on hats so we could see who could look the most horrible. Then we went home to Mother's to dinner. It was heavenly to be home with the family. They boiled around, cooking, telling what stinkers their various bosses were, sympathizing with me for having a doctor for a husband and generally being warm and comforting. Anne and Joan, Betty's small children, stuck to me, greedily asking for more stories about the 'knives and the bleed'...

All the family felt Sydney's gravitational pull, the impulse to turn in times of trouble to a wise and loving mother and a happy home. The description, and some of the language, is very similar to many scenes in Betty's *Anybody Can Do Anything*, published a year after Mary's book.

§

At the depth of the Depression, in 1933, one in four Americans was out of work but in Washington State it was higher than the national average at one in three. In Seattle and other cities where the jobless congregated, it was even higher. The Coroner reported that in 1932 fifty-eight out of the 190 suicides in Seattle's King County, the third highest suicide rate in the US, had been prompted by 'business reverses or unemployment'. Times were getting desperate.

For Betty, though, the year had started wonderfully with the publication of a two-part short story in Seattle's *Town Crier* magazine. She and Mary had previously tried to find a publisher for their joint tale *Sandra Surrenders*, the story of an unconventional sorority girl who nevertheless finds romance and marriage, which they thought at least as good as anything they heard on the radio. No publisher was interested. Now Betty had succeeded with her story *Their Families*. The magazine's Associate Editor was the family's longtime friend Margaret Bundy, now Margaret Bundy Callahan, by this time a writer and journalist who may well have been instrumental in getting Betty's story into print.

The tale concerns beautiful coppery-haired Judith, twenty-five, who has had a series of failed engagements because of objections to her unconventional family. She meets and falls in love with Peter and happily discovers that he has a family equally unconventional; all ends well, with a slight twist as both confess that they are not as unconventional as they make out.

The writing is not Betty MacDonald as we know it; the style is romantic and frothy, pretentious even, with only occasional touches of Betty's usual wit (an aunt appears with a noise like 'surf breaking on the beach'). However, the story is interesting for the material used from Betty's real life: already her subject was herself and her family, even in a work of fiction. Judith, who is probably modeled on the much engaged Mary, is given Betty's mother's ancestral name of Ten Eyck. The family consists of six brothers and sisters and a mother called Sydney who has a 'lovely, languid voice' and lounges around on sofas reading and smoking, forgetful that she has run out of money for food. The father is dead; one sister is divorced and has two little girls aged two and four who run around the house naked. Judith hides a gin stain on her dress under a sash; they have no money but set an elegant table; they read good literature aloud in the evenings; they are mutually supportive and fiercely loyal to each other. They even use Bardisms like *body-thinko*. All of the family are intellectual and creative but also more than a touch superior, looking down on those who are happy with suburban life – but secretly Judith rather yearns for simplicity. She confesses to Peter that she wants to have children and bake cookies on rainy Saturdays; he confesses to her that he rather enjoys his job as freight manager for a bus line. Overjoyed because neither is as unconventional as the rest of their families, they fall into each other's arms happily envisaging the suburban life ahead of them.

Their Families may not be quite on a par with Betty's other work, but the story is fascinating as a piece of juvenilia indicative of what was to come. And the picture painted of the family in the story – consciously intellectual, verging on the snobbish – may not have been too far from the Bards themselves. Family friend Margaret Bundy has this to say about the Bards:

> *Not the usual type of snob at all, but a peculiar type all their own. Social position and wealth meant nothing to the Bards, except in the most naïve, make-believe sort of way. Theirs was a snobbery based on personal attraction, and they were merciless towards those they regarded as uninteresting.*

Margaret believed that before Darsie Bard's death the family's lives were probably governed by conventional class distinctions but that afterwards, when the money was gone, they turned with characteristic insouciance to whatever illusions they could afford.

Not long after this Sydney, too, was suddenly earning money by her pen and making a unique contribution to the Bard finances, even though she was already fully occupied with the family's cooking, shopping and housekeeping and caring for Anne and Joan, who called their grandmother 'Margar' and their mother by her first name. (Betty later acknowledged that she had left the girls' upbringing to Sydney.)

The account in *Anybody Can Do Anything* is that Mary is working in radio advertising and one day sells a large department store on the idea of a daily radio serial, to be cast from the store's employees and to be directed by Mary herself. She states boldly that it's already written (a lie) and that she has left the script at the office. Rushing out to the nearest telephone, Mary begs Sydney to come up with a story which is both funny and suspenseful.

Sydney, an avid listener to radio soaps, or 'daily droolers', as Betty called them, dutifully sits down to try and write a compelling 15-minute drama – and succeeds.

Schuyler Square was launched in the *Seattle Post-Intelligencer's* 'What's What on the Air' column on 15 May 1933 as Mrs. D. C. Bard's 'thrilling new mystery serial'. The story followed six families living on a square, and the show went out live from a radio station inside the Rhodes Department Store in downtown Seattle as customers watched through a glass wall. Betty in *Anybody* wrote that thereafter Sydney sat late every night in the breakfast nook, drinking coffee and coughing her way through millions of cigarettes as she churned out the charming and funny story. In the book the show runs daily for the next year (in reality probably longer, according to Betty in other writing), and brings Sydney in twenty-five dollars a week, which makes a huge difference to the family income. Sydney was good at writing slogans, too: Betty wrote in an article that once she and Sydney each won a $50 prize in a slogan-writing contest, money which fortuitously arrived during a very bleak period when nobody in the house had a job.

Betty was only twenty-six when *Their Families* came out. It was her first ever published work, as far as is known, and she must have been thrilled. *Town Crier* probably didn't pay much, however, if anything; it was a literary magazine which folded only a few years later. There is no mention of the story's publication in *Anybody*; money remains tight and by February Betty is out of work and doing the rounds of the employment offices. She hates the hot, desperate smell of these places and can never conquer her fear of personnel managers, whose piercing glances and drilling questions crush Betty's fragile ego like an eggshell and in her own eyes expose her as completely unqualified to work anywhere. At least she now had a couple of years' experience, Betty thinks, when she applies for new jobs – only to be told that she is too old in her mid twenties. For general office work most companies wanted girls of eighteen.

Trying to sell advertising office to office like the super-confident Mary is a humiliating failure. Betty is too timid to ask to see the boss and is completely unconvincing in her sales spiel. She is scared to death all the time and doesn't really understand what she is selling. In the end even Mary acknowledges that her sister is not the salesperson type and should give up on the idea, so Betty goes back to pounding the streets for work along with the hordes of other unemployed and desperate people. Sometimes these so-called jobs are even dangerous: on one occasion she sees an advertisement for office workers and goes along for interview only to find the business is clearly a front for prostitution.

Slipping from one futureless job to another, Betty in *Anybody* is only just managing to make enough money to keep her and the girls afloat. To make matters worse, she owes money on a number of charge accounts opened the previous Christmas in the knowledge that the bills would not come in until February. Then comes February, and she can't pay. Betty lies awake at night in the bed she shares with Mary, tossing and turning and asking herself why she did it – she must have been crazy – what is she to do? She hates everything about living in the city and berates herself for ever leaving the farm.

After losing twelve pounds in weight, becoming very nervous and getting dark circles under her eyes, a solution suddenly seems to present itself. She borrows money from a loan company, at an exorbitant rate of interest and with hefty charges, and distributes it among the charge accounts with rash promises of more to come. But her usually temporary jobs, often paid in cash, do not make it easy to pay off large debts, and collectors on each of the charge accounts begin to harass her at her place of work. They appear in person or call her up, despite Betty trying to keep them from finding out where she is. She is desperately ashamed of owing money, and frightened. Then she gets behind on the payments to the loan company, and the company's own collectors start shouting at her in the streetcar or when she's going into a theater with a date. By mid 1933 Betty is at rock bottom: out of work, unable to pay her debts and hounded in public.

In July, luckily, her fortunes turned. When President Roosevelt succeeded Hoover in office in March 1933 the economy had nearly ground to a halt. Congress quickly passed a series of emergency measures to shore up the banking system and send urgently needed aid to the states. Huge public works projects were launched to create new jobs, and a new agency, the National Recovery Administration (NRA), was established to eliminate the existing cut-throat competition between industries. By a fluke, Betty suddenly landed a clerical job with the agency. The job was a government post which, for the first time, meant real security for Betty and the girls. She would get accumulated annual and sick leave and retirement funding. Not only that, but her debt problems were solved. In *Anybody*, Betty writes that the first week on the job so many debt collectors call her on the phone or come blustering into the office that she expects to be fired, but instead her new boss takes her down to the Federal Employees Union. They loan her the money to pay all her debts, and pay the bills on her behalf. She is free (apart from the little matter of needing to pay back the loan from the Union).

§

The aim of the National Recovery Administration was to bring industry, labor and government together so as to reduce destructive competition, and to help workers by setting minimum wages and maximum weekly hours. The agency, symbolized by a blue eagle, was popular with workers. Businesses that supported the NRA put the symbol in their shop windows and on their products. Membership was voluntary, but businesses that did not display the eagle were very often boycotted and only businesses with stickers could be awarded government contracts. Take-up was strong.

The NRA in Seattle was housed in the city's art deco Federal Office Building, which took up a whole block and to poverty-stricken Betty in *Anybody* looks like a very solid and respectable employer, unlike some of the dumps she has previously worked in. Here Betty starts as a temporary $4-a-day typist, feeling that at last she's working on the right side of the tracks. At first the work is boring and tiring, even though Betty thinks she will like a dull and monotonous job suited to what she assumes are her natural abilities. Eventually she begins to find the work intensely interesting and the period exciting. Her talents are recognized, despite her low opinion of herself. She quickly rises to a $120-a-month secretary, then to a clerk at $135 a month, and finally to labor adjuster at $1800 a year with her own secretary. In fact some reports suggest that Betty became the first female labor inspector in the whole of the US: an impressive career trajectory, if so, and evidence of Betty's sharp intelligence. Having a secretary was Betty's own criterion of success. At last, someone else taking down *her* thoughts; she was finally on the other end of the gun, she wrote.

Betty's success at the NRA must have done wonders for her confidence and self-esteem. Previously shy and unsure of herself, and all her life in Mary's flamboyant shadow, she at last came into her own. It's likely that her considerable intellect finally fastened onto a type of work demanding strategic thinking and an appreciation of the wider picture, and for the first time had a chance to flourish.

Blanche's new husband, Jock, was working in the same building as the NRA and when Blanche was there helping him out Betty would drop by to pick up her friend for coffee. Jock was amused when Betty addressed him as Simon Legree to imply he was working Blanche like the slave-driver in *Uncle Tom's Cabin*. The two old friends would swap their usual stories about work and friends and people they each knew. Betty was always fascinated by other people, no matter how dull, and deeply interested in how they lived their lives. She did distinguish between being interested, and actually liking. She never liked just anybody and needed people to be fascinating and witty enough to amuse her, or so boring as to be different; they needed to distinguish themselves enough to get her attention. It was the minutiae that so intrigued her. Blanche recalled how Betty would surprise her by remembering tiny details from Blanche's stories about other people, no matter how long the interval between their meetings. They would be chatting and Betty would suddenly ask, 'And how is poor little Patched

Coat?' This was a reference to an acquaintance of Blanche's who had been bragging about being taken to fabulous places by her terrific boyfriend, until someone in the boyfriend's office had revealed that the man was married and that his wife came to the office in a shabby old patched coat. Blanche had also told Betty about a friend who met a new man she hoped to marry because they had so much in common, such as liking to fold towels into thirds on the rack. Some time later Betty asked if 'those towel-folders' had ever married, adding that if they ever had a quarrel they could always make it up with a towel-folding session.

When Blanche began teaching, one of her fellow teachers used to hike her skirt far above her knees when sitting opposite the handsome headmaster at the teachers' meeting, and Blanche would occasionally point it out to her. The woman would pull it down a quarter-inch and say 'Thanks, Blanche.' Having heard the story, Betty would sometimes ask, 'Is 'Thanks, Blanche' still riding her skirts high?' (When Betty's sister Alison heard about this years later, she suddenly understood where the phrase had come from. The whole family had been saying 'Thanks, Blanche' to each other for years without knowing its origin.) Then there was the time Blanche demonstrated to Betty the way she made sure she always hung her husband Jock's suits with the sleeves sharply creased and all lined up after he had complained that Blanche left them askew. Betty joked that he sounded like Father Bear asking who had been eating his porridge, and thereafter asked Blanche at intervals if she was keeping Father Bear's creases smooth.

Betty in her turn told Blanche of a co-worker who was attempting to get a man to marry her. Betty happened to overhear the friend talking dreamily to the man about their possible future, which the woman envisaged with three stalwart sons and a Dalmatian at the man's feet. From then on Betty kept Blanche posted on the romance of 'Three Stalwart Sons', Betty's new nickname for the friend.

All of this is just mere detail in the scheme of things but as Blanche commented, Betty thrived on observing people and their foibles. In her opinion Betty's memory for small detail lent the commonplace a measure of significance. It was the ordinariness of everyday life that Betty loved and that drew the two together during their long friendship.

Mike

By this time, of course, Betty was making her own friends and not just inheriting Mary's. In *Anybody* she sometimes meets a man she likes, although there is never enough money to go anywhere and get any privacy. Love affairs have to be conducted in front of the fire, reading poetry and listening to music on the radio, or walking up to view the lights of the city reflected in the reservoir. Little came of these romances in the early years of Betty's return from the ranch. Mary once confided to Blanche that Betty would have a hard time finding a man as smart as she was. When Betty was going out with one of Seattle's most brilliant electrical engineers, Mary worried that Betty, not the type to hide her intelligence, would have him thinking that he couldn't put two wires together.

If not exactly a grand passion, one of Betty's more memorable men friends around this time was Mike Gordon, a man of over seventy. They first met in 1934 and Betty later wrote an article about Mike for the *Reader's Digest* series 'The Most Unforgettable Character I've Met.'

According to this account Mike is at least a foot shorter than Betty, looks like a little troll, and speaks with an odd accent combining traces of Swedish, Scots and Greek. With such a disparity in their ages it doesn't occur to Betty that Mike could consider himself as a possible date, but Mike immediately sets about wooing her with extravagant but strange gifts. Instead of flowers or candy, Mike sends her a side of beef or several hundred cans of pea soup or four dozen pairs of nylons, all slightly irregular in size and shade. He's also extremely generous to Betty's family.

As always with Betty it's tempting to assume that at least some of this is exaggerated for comic effect, but her old friend Blanche attested to the reality of Mike and his strange wooing. A photograph in Blanche's memoir shows Mike and Betty against a backdrop of Eastern Washington hills, Betty towering over Mike with her arm around his diminutive shoulders. Visiting the Bards' house the first Christmas after Betty had met her eccentric suitor, Blanche could barely step into the living room for all the presents under the tree, and they even spilled into the dining room and half way up the stairs to the bedrooms. Betty waved her hand over it all and simply said, 'Mike.' Towering above the beautifully wrapped packages were two shiny bicycles for Anne and Joan.

Blanche once asked Betty if she felt at all obligated to Mike for all he did for her. Betty answered that all she had to do was reach down and pat him on the cheek and make him laugh a lot.

In the article about him Betty writes that all Mike's friends had to be either *wealty* or *prrrrrrrominent,* as he pronounced it. People who are not his friends are *damn appleknockers,* the term used for the transient workers who came to harvest apples in Eastern Washington where

Mike lived and conducted his successful lumber business. All of Mike's friends suffer from his excessive gift-giving, which Betty eventually finds irritating – but not Anne and Joan, strangely enough. Mike would deliver a ton of whatever item a friend had inadvertently let slip he or she liked, although always it's the wrong sort or a different type that Mike himself is fond of. He throws extravagant parties and picnics that are tightly scripted and have to be followed to the letter or he complains bitterly. For Betty this bossiness is almost unbearable. Nevertheless, Mike's strange courtship continues for another eight years and during all that time Betty keeps trying to think of things to do for Mike and ways to repay his generosity. She makes him sketches and sends him pictures, and is forever on the lookout for something she can afford that Mike doesn't already have sixty of.

When *The Egg and I* came out many years later, Betty made reference to Mike and his ways in the front of Blanche's copy:

This is a copy that I autographed during the flurry – I'm not trying to be prrrrrrrominent – but I am wealty – from your oldest school chum – Betty.

§

On 8 March 1935, when Betty's divorce finally came through, she was once again a free woman. But Bob had not paid support for the previous two years and had never paid the costs of the divorce as mandated. Betty had to go on fighting to get her money, even after the final decree. In September Bob was ordered back before the judge, found guilty of contempt of court and given a suspended sentence of thirty days in the County Jail. By this time he owed his employer money and was borrowing from friends and relatives, including his father.

Betty was again in need of money: she knew she was just about to lose her steady government job at the NRA. The US Supreme Court had declared that the law providing for the NRA was unconstitutional, as it infringed the separation of powers under the United States Constitution. The organization was to close down on 31 December and Betty would be out of work yet again. On Christmas Eve both she and Bob were in court once more as she fought on for the support he owed her. Bob offered just $15, a meager sum loaned by his father Otis (a witness at Bob and Betty's wedding in 1927), who was urging him to support his children. The court asked Betty to accept the payment and arranged a further hearing for January 1936. Bob's sentence continued to be suspended.

Come January and they were both back in court. Clearly losing patience, the judge observed that Bob appeared to be 'in need of a stimulus' and ordered him to serve ten days of his suspended sentence. He subsequently modified this, ordering Bob to pay $10 instead. The judge's unusual phrasing made it into the local press. 'Ex-Husband Pays Family $10.00 Under 'Added Stimulus',' declared a small item in the *Seattle Times*. Misreporting or misunderstanding the sequence of events, the newspaper summed it up as insurance salesman Robert Heskett being forced to choose between ten days in prison or paying $10 in support of his ex-wife Mrs. Elizabeth Heskett and her two daughters, aged seven and eight. Bob paid up. The case would be heard again in February.

Meanwhile Betty as a government worker had fortunately been able to transfer to the US Treasury

Department, starting at her new post in mid February. However, despite the seniority she had attained at the NRA, she had to start all over again from the bottom at a lower salary. To make matters worse she had broken her leg or ankle while skiing, which she had never liked in the first place, and had to spend her first days on the new job with her leg in a cast. This meant she was unable to attend the February hearing, but then neither did Bob. He had run through two attorneys by now and was on his third, and a female friend (from whom he was in the habit of borrowing money) explained to this last attorney that he would not be appearing because he had left the jurisdiction of the court. Another warrant for Bob's arrest was issued, again for contempt of court.

In *Anybody* Betty's first post at the Treasury is in a department which deals with supplies and contracts for another part of President Roosevelt's recovery program, the Works Progress Administration or WPA (later to become the Works Projects Administration). This was a nationwide program of building bridges, roads, public buildings, public parks, airports, and swimming pools to provide employment for needy workers; new projects were identified by local government and the federal government footed the bill. Jobs with the WPA were only open to the unemployed and, in order to spread the work around, individual families could only have one member at a time working for the program. Times were still hard and applications in Seattle had flooded in; the WPA was soon employing thousands of people in the area. Betty's job as described in *Anybody* is dealing with bids for the various WPA projects, which she initially finds difficult. From this section she progresses very slowly to contracts, which is frustratingly bureaucratic and even busier. In the end she just resigns herself to the infinitesimally slow ways of government and begins to relax enough to feel happy in the job.

The WPA carried out publicity on its own behalf, including employing photographers to document conditions in the Depression; one of these was the young Eudora Welty, later to win fame as a great writer of the American South. As Eudora traveled throughout Mississippi taking her hundreds of photographs, many of which were only published after several decades, she also gathered material for her highly acclaimed stories of the Deep South. Years later, when Betty herself was a writer, these two old WPA hands were to meet.

A photograph taken some time in 1936 by the Bards' theater artist friend Florence James shows a smiling Betty and Blanche enjoying themselves on a trip to Victoria. (Both are dressed rather formally but the look is enlivened by big Minnie Mouse shoes – clearly in fashion at the time as each is wearing a similar pair.) Despite the lack of support from Bob, life for Betty was definitely getting easier as the Depression receded and she made her way up in government service.

Then, suddenly, calamity struck.

Betty and the Plague

BY 1937 both Mary and Cleve had married and left the family home. The Bards' dearly loved grandmother Gammy had died in 1936 in Boulder, Colorado, where she had gone to live with relatives several years previously. Betty, ten- and nine-year-old Anne and Joan, her mother Sydney, younger sisters Dede and Alison, and family friend and honorary sister Madge were all still living in the shingled house in the University District. Betty was gainfully employed in government service and happy in her work. Money, although tight, was no longer such a problem.

Then, gradually, Betty realized she was feeling ill. In her account in *The Plague and I* she has a series of coughs and colds, vague pains in her back and lungs and absolutely no energy. She wakes up tired, feeds herself coffee and cigarettes to get started and then snatches lie-downs on a hard bench in the restroom at work just to keep going. Each successive cold leaves her thinner and more tired. She can't understand it. Betty as a child was delicate and had contracted a number of childhood diseases, but as an adolescent she had turned as plump and healthy as the rest of the family, despite Gammy's dire warnings about catarrh, consumption and leprosy lurking just around the corner. In fact Gammy would caution against catching consumption, or tuberculosis, with a special relish. When the children were little she would read aloud the account of Beth's fatal illness in *Little Women* and tell them how Robert Louis Stevenson had died of the disease; she would warn the children's father that his insistence on cold baths at five in the morning would drive the children straight into consumption, and advise the teenaged Betty that trying to lose weight would end the same way.

Despite these ominous warnings the children had all grown up hale and hearty. The Bards generally paid no attention to minor ailments and disliked talk of illness; they thought people who went on about their operations were big bores. The family would label any of their number who complained about their health, if the condition was not actually accompanied by a serious temperature, as a 'big sicko' or 'big saddo'. Now Betty was rapidly becoming both.

Despite Gammy's early warnings it never occurred to Betty that she had tuberculosis. She was nearly thirty years old, had been married and divorced and had two children and knew plenty about life, but she just knew nothing about tuberculosis or its symptoms. She wrote that she was operating under the family assumption that she had her health, and in any case she thought the only symptoms of tuberculosis were a dry hacking cough and seeing flecks of blood on a clean white handkerchief delicately touched to the lips.

In *Plague* she embarks on a series of consultations with various specialists, but never tells each one the entire array of her apparently unrelated symptoms because she feels ashamed of the long list of little things wrong with her. Each of the doctors pats her shoulder and sends her away without a diagnosis. She even has a physical for insurance purposes and is pronounced fit and healthy enough for several thousand dollars' worth. In September she begins to suffer with hemorrhoids so she calls Mary, who sends her to her pathologist husband Clyde Jensen. Believing that pathology related to the entire human body, this time Betty relays all of her symptoms, including even her nervousness and insomnia. Clyde listens carefully, examines her, tests her sputum (coughed-up phlegm or mucus), has her lungs x-rayed and passes her to a chest specialist.

The specialist diagnoses pulmonary tuberculosis. He tells Betty she needs complete bedrest at a sanatorium, probably for at least a year, and that she is contagious.

Betty is struck with fear. Having read *The Magic Mountain*, Thomas Mann's novel about patients in a tuberculosis sanatorium, she knows that these are places in the Swiss Alps where people go to die. Everyone she's ever heard of with the disease has died of it. She will undoubtedly be in excellent company, she writes in *Plague*, but she doesn't want to die.

She asks about the cost of a sanatorium: if she's in a hospital and not working, she can't pay for treatment. Mary's husband offers to write a letter to an endowed sanatorium in Seattle that is free to anyone with the illness and unable to pay. There's a waiting list, but Clyde tells the shaken Betty that mothers with small children are usually admitted without delay.

As soon as she gets home Betty is put to bed in Sydney's room where there's a fire blazing in the fireplace and infinite love and sympathy from the family. She feels almost happy to know, finally, what is wrong with her: that she really is ill, not just lazy and without ambition, and that her terrible lassitude and pointless fatigue are due to disease. She can legitimately be a big, no-sense-of-humor saddo. She coughs all night and enjoys doing it.

What a pity Gammy wasn't still alive to hear the diagnosis, Betty wrote. It would have given her such satisfaction.

Firland

Tuberculosis (TB) is a highly contagious disease caused by the bacterium *Mycobacterium tuberculosis*. Tuberculosis typically attacks the lungs, but can also affect other parts of the body. It is spread through the air when people with an active TB infection cough or sneeze and transmit respiratory fluids through the air to others. The most common form is pulmonary tuberculosis, the type Betty had, but the bacteria can also infect the kidneys, bones, and intestines, as well as the lymph nodes. The classic symptoms of active TB infection are a chronic cough with blood-tinged sputum, fever, night sweats, and weight loss (the latter giving rise to the old name of 'consumption' for TB). Before a cure became possible, tuberculosis was usually fatal and was nicknamed the White Plague.

Firland sanatorium, Seattle's municipal tuberculosis hospital, had opened north of the city in 1911 to treat what was then Seattle's leading cause of death. In downtown Seattle a Health Department Free Clinic screened people for the disease. Patients with financial means were directed towards private sanatoria while poorer patients were admitted to Firland, usually after being placed on a lengthy waiting list, as only 250 patients could be treated at any one time. The Medical Director of the sanatorium was a Dr. Robert Stith, whose own mother had died of tuberculosis.

The sanatorium gave priority to those who seemed curable and would only admit sufferers who had lived in

Seattle for at least a year. As Mary's husband Dr. Jensen had indicated, tubercular women who had dependent children were often admitted immediately without having to wait their turn, and their children could also be admitted and given preventive treatment. Dr. Stith had absolute authority to decide who would be admitted; he tried to use available funds and limited beds wisely and to admit only those who were 'worth saving', as he put it. Medical expenses for patients admitted to Firland were paid by the Seattle Department of Health and the State of Washington.

Firland, 1927
Courtesy of the Seattle Municipal Archives, item number 2655

Treatment was still extremely limited in the 1930s when Betty was stricken with the disease and consisted chiefly of a prolonged period in bed. Firland's dictum for its patients was absolute rest: 'Rest – more rest – and still more rest. Rest is the keynote. Rest for the body, rest for the mind. Rest from involuntary as well as voluntary activity forms the basis on which the cure is built.' Today TB can mostly be cured with antibiotics in a matter of just months but at that time the only possibility was complete rest, often for years, to allow tubercular lesions to heal by themselves. Some patients were also treated surgically using techniques designed to keep the lungs more still; as tubercular lungs could not be subjected to general anesthesia, this thoracic surgery had to be performed under local anesthesia only. But even with total rest and surgery there were no guarantees.

Firland's strict rules were constantly reiterated by the medical staff, and patients were continually warned that the numerous tubercular patients on the waiting list were anxious to take their places if they could not comply. Instructional pamphlets or little slips containing uplifting thoughts ('If you must be blue, be a bright blue') arrived on the patients' dinner trays. The nurses also trained their patients in hygiene, as a number of unhygienic practices were still common in Seattle at the time. People did not necessarily hold their hands over their mouths when coughing or sneezing and some were still spitting on the floor, despite legislation against spitting in public in place since 1898. Deadly bacilli in saliva and sputum then spread tuberculosis, just as Betty claims in *Plague*: she believes she has been infected by a contagious co-worker who repeatedly coughed in her face. As for the nurses themselves, the nursing was decidedly unpleasant. There was the infectious sputum, the lung hemorrhaging and the frequent vomiting, especially during mealtimes. Despite precautions many nurses became infected, and, like the patients, some died.

§

In *The Plague and I* Betty takes us through her long months of incarceration at Firland ('The Pines' in the book), seven of them on complete bedrest. First comes the unsympathetic, impersonal assessment at the downtown clinic in Seattle, a depressing place which shares a building with the police station, the city jail, an emergency hospital and a venereal disease clinic. On the way up to the clinic Betty is convinced that everyone else in the elevator is a crook or a prostitute but they all file out, looking sad, at the TB clinic just like her. The nurses' manner at the clinic is cold and unpleasant, which comes as a surprise to Betty after her experience of kind and motherly nursing when in hospital having her children. It's later explained to her that as the Firland nurses needed to enforce the strict regime at the sanatorium they were trained to remain completely impersonal, which Betty fully understands and finds helpful to know when she is eventually a patient.

Before going in Betty is naturally worried about how long she will have to remain. In *Plague* the chest specialist guesses at a year's stay but also adds 'or longer', which could mean anything from another month to ten years. Dr Stith also tells her that with her red hair, energy and impatience, the discipline at the sanatorium would be extra hard. 'Prognosis – doubtful' is written on her notes.

The day of departure for the sanatorium dawns. Betty tries to play it down for the children's sake; people who packed up their troubles in their old kit-bag and remained inanely cheerful through adversity made the Bards want to be sick, she wrote, but equally the family didn't want to be too tragic about the whole thing. Nevertheless, she is devastated as she watches Anne and Joan waving her goodbye. She is driven to Firland by the family and is given a bleak reception. Another impersonal nurse – or just plain thoroughly disagreeable, in Betty's view – takes her details and gives her several papers to sign. The nurse also hands over a book of sanatorium rules and the visiting regulations, which include the warning that if her visitors come too early, stay too late, are noisy, break rules or exceed the allotted three in number, then her visiting privileges will be removed for an indefinite period of time. A maximum of three adult visitors are allowed on Thursday and Sunday afternoons for two hours; children are allowed to visit only once a month, for ten minutes (Firland also stipulated that children had to stay at the door and not touch the patient). After this warm welcome Florence Nightingale directs Betty and the family to a silent waiting room, whence Betty is eventually removed in a wheelchair after emotional farewells. 'I can't bear to say goodbye to you, Betsy,' her mother sighs.

Before entering the ward she is subjected to a bath in boiling water and disinfectant and a further recitation of the rules: patients must not read, write, talk, laugh, sing, or reach; patients must lie still and relax. As she lies in the bath another of the grim nurses examines the contents of Betty's suitcases and explodes with righteous indignation when she comes across some innocent bottles of cough medicine and aspirin.

'Patients must <u>never</u> take medicines without the Doctor's permission. No patient of the sanatorium <u>ever has medicine</u> of any kind whatsoever in his possession. Patients are <u>never</u> allowed to choose own medicines. These,' she held up the cough medicine and aspirin as if they were Home Cure for Syphilis and Quick Aborto, 'will have to be sent home or <u>destroyed</u>. These extra sweaters, these bed jackets, all your clothes, books, writing materials and <u>handkerchiefs</u> (her

disdain of this last filthy habit-forming article was tremendous) will have to go through fumigation and be sent home.'

After this processing Betty is finally placed in a clammy bed in a square ward with four beds, one in each corner, and large, curtainless windows opened wide to the elements. She is not allowed a hot water bottle, as they are only given out from 1 October (this is the very end of September). Her life as a TB patient has begun.

Newly admitted patients began their time at Firland lying motionless in the Bedrest Hospital and, just as Betty wrote in *Plague*, reading, writing, and talking were not allowed. Except to produce a morning sputum sample, patients had to suppress their coughs for fear of sparking a coughing mania among other patients and to avoid aggravating their fragile healing lungs. Even reaching for nearby items was prohibited. Other activities considered harmful included 'letter writing, reading, dolling up; for example, curling the hair, painting the face, etc., letting the mind dwell on any subject which hurries circulation'. Fresh air was considered crucial to the cure and screened windows were kept wide open all year round. Plenty of nourishing food was on offer and patients were expected to eat well to build up their strength.

In *Plague* Betty describes her first few weeks at Firland in moving but comic detail. To start with, her thoughts are gloomy and she has problems remembering how eager she had been to enter Firland, how grateful to the Medical Director for allowing her to jump the queue, how wonderful it was to receive completely free treatment. She is cold and lonely and misses Anne and Joan, who are being looked after by her mother and the rest of the family. She is not allowed to read, or write, or talk. She takes us through the long, tedious process of each day: the explosive awakening at six each morning as the wash-water girls snap on the lights and jerk the patients out of sleep with the crash of their jugs and basins; the tiny amount of water given out for washing and teeth-cleaning; the disgusting coughing and spitting all over the hospital in accordance with prescribed procedure (presumably to produce their sputum samples); the temperature-taking, the bed-pan rounds, the meals, which are good, if often cold, and the two hours each day of strictly observed rest which Betty initially finds extremely difficult. There is also, of course, the complete lack of privacy twenty-four hours a day. Betty likens this to adjusting to an arranged marriage but without the curiosity or the sex.

The routine is enlivened only by visiting day on Sundays, bath days once a week, a hair-wash every four to six weeks and weigh-ins on the last day of each month. For her visitors Betty puts on lots of make-up, which she suspects makes her look like an 'old sick Madam', but raises her spirits. On bath days, disappointingly, Betty learns that bedrest patients are taken to a bathroom and washed on a bed by a nurse: tub baths are not allowed. On weighing days the nurses push a large pair of scales into each ward and the patients are helped up from bed to be weighed, each holding their breath in case they have lost rather than gained. Losing weight signified a backward slide but gaining weight meant at least a foothold on the climb back to health. The despair in the ward felt by those who have lost weight is palpable.

Writing about the nine months she spent at the sanatorium Betty achieves a nice balance between extracting the maximum humor from the situation – the other patients, the nurses ('Granite Eyes' and 'Gravy

Face'), the routine, the boredom of lying there doing nothing, the cold and discomfort in the drafty wards – and the genuine terror she experienced as the victim of a then potentially fatal disease. There was no guarantee at the time that she would ever emerge from Firland alive, let alone cracking jokes. However, others have attested to the fact that her sense of humor really did sustain her and that her unfailing ability to see the funny side was a surprise, and mostly a delight, to her fellow sufferers. One of these was 'Kimi', a young Japanese girl who in reality was Monica Sone, the Seattle-born daughter of Japanese immigrants. Monica wrote about her months at Firland in her own autobiography, describing Betty's fluff of copper-bright hair, her easy laugh and the crisp humor which relieved the drabness of their highly regimented existence. Monica was devastated to have tuberculosis and couldn't understand how Betty could seem so cheerful. When the two eventually shared a small room together, Monica had at first planned not to intrude on Betty's privacy beyond the necessary minimum, but found trying to remain distant from Betty was like trying to ignore a blaze of fireworks. She could not remain untouched by Betty's brilliant wit and her irresistible zest for living, and felt as if Betty was bodily dragging her up into bright sunlight from a pit of self-pity. Every morning Betty would burst through Monica's groggy sleep with a 'Good morning' in Japanese (learned from Monica), and a funny comment to get the day going. For Monica, Betty made the long, long hours at the sanatorium bearable; for Betty, her friend's wit and resignation were a vital support in her worst hours. One of Betty's acid tests for friendship became whether someone would be pleasant to have TB with.

Another witness to Betty's constant good cheer was her faithful school friend Blanche, who came to visit about a month after Betty entered Firland. As she approached the ward she could hear laughing and talking. The nurse showing her in started to smile too. 'Listen to Betty,' she said. 'She keeps us all laughing. Most of her room-mates love her – although one sensitive girl had to be moved because she couldn't take Betty's sense of humor' (an incident not mentioned in *The Plague and I*). Betty introduced Blanche to her fellow sufferers and everyone started to talk at once. They had many little in-jokes and favorite characters at the institution to laugh about, and anecdotes that made life at the deadly serious Firland seem one long riot.

However, laughter was in fact taboo at Firland because of what it could do to healing lungs. It's obvious in *Plague* that her jokey behavior was disapproved of by the staff and, while it might have kept her and those around her sane, the reality was that she was jeopardizing her health. In any case, beneath the wisecracks Betty makes clear in *Plague* that, certainly at first, she is always grimly aware of where she is and how it could end; she is outwardly cheerful but inwardly often thinking the worst. Betty's children were totally dependent on her and much of her internal brooding inevitably revolves around their future and what would happen if she died. She had lost her own father at about their age. *The Plague and I*, though funny and immensely enjoyable, is the most somber of Betty's books.

Fortunately, she began to recover almost immediately. In *Plague*, after only two weeks of complete bedrest, she has gained weight and begun to feel better. The resting has grown easier and through the long quiet days she has been able to relax more and more. There comes a night when she sleeps the whole night through and the next morning doesn't cough at all when she wakes up. She has a new sense of well-being and a feeling of energy, feels perfectly well and has lost some of the depression and feeling of terrible foreboding. Betty begins to think about the future with some hope of actually getting well. Naturally it then drives her insane to lie hour after hour, day after day doing nothing, but she has to continue following the prescribed program. Inevitably this starts to produce a dreadful restlessness and irritability. And, in line with Firland policy, Betty is told nothing about her good progress, which might have helped her state of mind. Despite regular x-rays and tests, nothing was ever revealed to the patient.

From October onwards it begins to rain and rain and when it isn't raining there is mist and fog; because of the open windows, everything, including hair and bedclothes, becomes damp and clammy. The sanatorium, always cold, becomes colder still. Patients all wear several pairs of woolen socks and are so wrapped up in sweaters and scarves and hoods and mittens that they look like bundles of old clothes, but they are all still cold all the time. The heating is now on in the building but with the constantly open windows it goes nowhere. The cold makes the patients irritable and snappish, especially Betty (in her own estimation). Food, which at first had been hot at least at lunchtime, becomes progressively colder as the winter advances. Meals are brought from the kitchens via long icy tunnels and any heat can't survive the journey, although the food itself continues to be excellent.

Because a shadow on her right lung clears very quickly it becomes possible for Betty to be given an artificial pneumothorax, a common surgical method used at Firland to arrest tuberculosis. This was based on the theory that a flattened lung would heal more quickly. Compression was effected by the introduction of gas or filtered air into the pleural cavity between the chest wall and the lung, and refills of the air were given at regular and then increasingly spaced intervals, and could be continued for a number of years.

In *Plague* Betty is told nothing about what is going to happen to her and as she waits in a side room she is so scared she is practically in a coma. It proves to be an unpleasant experience. In fact artificial pneumothorax was not without its dangers, although it is reported to have helped cure or extend the lives of many at the time. Having survived the ordeal Betty climbs back into bed with a terrific, overwhelming desire for a cigarette (which, of course, she had been obliged to give up on entering Firland).

In mid November Betty is moved to a room by herself, possibly because there has been too much laughing and talking with her former room-mate 'Kimi', and she loses her feeling of high spirits and growing good health and spends much of her time longing for the children and thinking about dying. She appears not to have had any consolation from religion at this critical point in her life. She had been brought up as Episcopalian, and used to take the girls to church when they were young but may not have had any deep religious feeling. Elsewhere in *Plague* she does describe hearing the soft murmurs of the 'sweet-faced, gentle Catholic Fathers' going from room to room blessing the patients, and wishing that they would stop at her bed: only the Catholic Church appeared to her to have the true feeling of religion, she wrote. Nevertheless she appears to have been without the comfort of strongly held belief that other patients may well have called upon. When asked by a nurse if something is troubling her, Betty answers truthfully that she hates being alone, longs for her children and thinks about death. The nurse is horrified and orders Betty to have pleasant cheerful thoughts. She gathers herself together and from then on, as she lies there through the long sad days, cold and lonely, Betty consciously tries to assemble cheery thoughts to keep her going when she is wakeful in the night.

At Firland, once a patient's daily sputum samples indicated that he or she was no longer contagious, the sanatorium gradually began testing the patient's strength. Those who showed signs of recovery through weight gain, improved chest x-ray, negative sputum samples, and normal temperature and pulse were given 'time up', which meant they could sit up in bed for a given number of minutes, and then gradually a number of hours each day. If a patient showed no sign of relapse, additional privileges such as reading and writing time and, eventually, permission to walk down the hall to the bathroom followed. By December 1937 Betty in *Plague* has at last been moved back to a two-bed cubicle (perhaps for her good behavior all on her own) and has graduated to one hour's reading time a day and is taking pneumothorax only once a week. She is also colder than she has ever been. The patients' bedpans and water glasses freeze solid each night and they all wear woolen mittens and woolen hoods even at meal-times.

After all these months Betty has become institutionalized: she knows the hospital routine by heart, what's going to happen hour by hour and minute by minute. No longer thrilled even by a big holiday like Thanksgiving, she knows each day only as bath day, 'gas' day, fluoroscope (a type of x-ray) day, visiting day, supply day or store day, when patients received items such as toiletries and the like ordered from Firland's store. She is aware that this is down to a combination of the divorce from normal living and the self-centeredness of the invalid. Although at first vitally interested in her visitors' stories of life on the outside, gradually these tales became less and less real. The only reality is the sanatorium – its patients, staff and happenings. This makes time move unbelievably slowly and Betty becomes ever more irritable as she lies there just waiting for the hours to pass. Her room-mate at this point is a very obedient, inspirational patient who is so annoying that Betty lies awake in the long dark nights listening hopefully for her breathing to stop.

The period for bedrest patients to start engaging in occupational therapy, go to one of Firland's movie showings, read books, and have time up – if they were judged well enough after a chest examination – was three months. In *Plague* Betty reaches this milestone at the end of December, and she is wheeled away to be examined just as she is telling herself that she will be in the sanatorium for the rest of her life but that at least she will go through menopause under medical supervision. After a thorough appraisal she is told she can have three hours' time up and one hour of occupational therapy time a day, leaving her almost hysterical with joy. However, she is dismayed, to the point of tears, by the occupational therapy activities on offer: knitting, crocheting, tatting, or embroidery. She had thought that the therapy would be useful work, something she could do to support herself and Anne and Joan if she wasn't strong enough to return to regular work after her release. None of the sorry objects she is shown as samples of what she could do would ever bring in money but she is told that the idea is more to add interest to the patients' days, to keep them occupied and release tension. Morosely, Betty chooses tatting, a form of lacemaking with a shuttle. It makes listening to the radio and time up more pleasant and so she gets on with it.

When her time up, which is increased by five minutes a day, reaches one hour, she is wheeled to the porch morning and evening to join the other time-uppers. Bundled in everything they own they sit in reclining chairs and in the mornings do their knitting or tatting with frozen fingers. The evenings are too dark so they just sit and shiver. Betty's mother is delighted about Betty's time up and occupational therapy and brings her in a thick book of tatting instructions. Betty looks at the attractive illustrations of collars and cuffs and tablecloths, reads the instructions and works hard, but for a long time can only produce small 'pustules' of grayish white thread.

Occupational therapy also allowed the medical staff to keep observing patients' strength. Firland offered leatherwork, photography classes, a woodshop, a machine shop, a print shop, a beauty parlor, a full domestic arts department and even a volunteer fire department, all staffed by recovering patients. Those engaged on these activities were continually monitored to guard against relapse, and if temperature or pulse increased they were put back to bed. Those with eight hours up, the maximum time allowed, were still expected to spend the remaining sixteen of the twenty-four hours at rest.

Patients with the requisite skills – like Betty, who could type – could also help produce Firland's inhouse magazine *Pep* (later called *Firland Magazine*), which sold subscriptions to help towards the costs of occupational therapy. The aim of the magazine was to educate and inform patients and to raise morale. There were columns on famous tuberculosis sufferers, a joke column called 'Your Sputum', and news of former patients. There was frequent urging to STOP and REST. Birthdays, admissions, and discharges were listed; those who had died were listed as discharged, which at times was as many as one-third of the list. Patients back in the community often continued to subscribe to the magazine in order to keep up with their old friends.

Recovering patients also delivered mail or library books round the wards, pushed wheelchairs or worked in the dining hall. They carried out practical and useful tasks such as sewing surgical gowns and linens and rolling bandages, or delivering items to fellow patients' beds from the Firland Exchange Store. Outdoors they could work on the Firland Farm, which provided the institution with vegetables, fruit, eggs, poultry, and pork; the farm even raised guinea pigs for use in Firland laboratory experiments. There were the beautiful grounds to walk in and a miniature golf course. Coincidentally, some of the land had been cleared by men put to work by the Works Progress Administration, the job creation agency Betty had done work for while at the Treasury. In *Plague* Betty's eventual job during this recovery period is to work as one of the dreaded wash-water girls who crash the bed-rest patients so hideously awake each morning with their jugs and basins. For Betty it's a point of honor to make damned sure every patient gets enough water to wash and clean their teeth with. Some of her old friends in the Bedrest Hospital are so much worse it makes her cry.

Betty is getting better and taking the first steps towards normality, but more treatment is to come: having her 'bands' cut. This was pneumolysis, the snipping of large adhesions between the lung and the pleural membrane. If a patient had received artificial pneumothorax, strong adhesions like this could hamper a proper collapse of the lung and therefore delay healing. Not surprisingly the procedure was another unpleasant experience, again carried out with only local anesthetic, although Betty does have an injection of morphine. Unfortunately she is allergic to it (her warning is ignored) and instead of dulling the pain the drug makes her highly alert and nervous. In *Plague* she also makes the mistake of wearing mascara and the discomfort from the stinging, running mascara in the hot operating theater proves far greater torture than the procedure itself.

Betty was fortunate to have closed pneumolysis, meaning a less invasive puncture in the chest wall through which to do the cutting, instead of an open pneumolysis, which was a removal of portions of the ribs to get at more extensive adhesions. Even so, a variety of mishaps were possible during the closed pneumolysis, including cardiac arrest due to stimulation of the vagus nerve or even death from hemorrhage following the accidental cutting of a vein. There were many accidents and poor results from this procedure during that era. Eventually, from the 1940s onwards, the procedure was totally replaced by drug therapy. Betty, luckily, survived. As it was, she wrote in *Plague* that following the procedure she experienced a peculiar scrunchy feeling in her wrist, which turned out to be a bubble of air in her veins from the badly administered hypodermic of morphine. She was given a sedative and luckily the air dissipated before the bubble, or embolism, reached her heart with potentially fatal consequences.

A Firland inmate making good progress would finally be moved into a ward for ambulant patients, where he or she enjoyed greater freedom and could take meals in the dining room rather than on trays in bed. As always, staff were instructed never to discuss a patient's case with them directly, so they never knew exactly where they were in their recovery and when additional privileges might be granted. Each new privilege gave rise to growing hope and elation. Betty's condition continued to improve and in March 1939, at six hours up and having gained twenty pounds in weight since she entered, a chest examination showed that she was ready to become an ambulant patient. In *Plague* her bed is moved and to her delight her new accommodation, which she shares with one other room-mate, has its own warm dressing-room and a private toilet. They can fill up their own hot water bottles to their hearts' content and have real baths in a tub instead of blanket baths. Betty is ecstatic at the change of location and the chance to go to something so normal as a movie – and in the company of those now strange animals, men, from whom she has been segregated for so many months.

There was very strict separation of the sexes at the hospital. At the time, tuberculosis was popularly supposed to be accompanied by a frenetic sex drive; at Firland any thoughts or activities relating to sex were forbidden, and Director Stith guarded against any possibility of assignation by enforcing a deliberate isolation. He placed older, more mature nurses to care for the male patients while the only men regularly seen on the women's bedrest floor were the doctors and several trusted older ambulant patients who cranked the heads of the beds up for meals. Ambulant patients joined separate cafeteria lines for men and women, ate on opposite sides of the dining room, and sat on opposite sides of the aisle at the monthly movie shows.

In the Ambulant Hospital there was far less nurse supervision and the patients could talk freely. Within two weeks Betty is no longer taken in a wheelchair to the dining-room but is going to and fro under her own steam. Heaven. In *Plague* Betty's family are naturally delighted with her progress, if taken aback by her staggering change in weight when they come to visit her in the Ambulant Hospital and see her out of bed for the first time in months. Betty wrote that the insidious piling up of superfluous flesh was the penalty she had paid for her well-contained tuberculosis germs.

She is doing well, and after a month in the Ambulant Hospital another chest examination shows she is ready for eight hours up and can start wearing her own clothes. In June she becomes eligible for a Town leave, a chance to make a longed-for visit home. The leave is finally granted by the Medical Director but with a special addendum: Betty's attitude does not warrant a Town leave, she is told, and if she does not materially change her behavior the only Town leave granted again might be a permanent one. Presumably Betty's irrepressible sense of humor and sociability were still getting her into trouble. In *Plague*, after a wonderful, emotional time at home with Anne and Joan and the family, during which the 'very foreign atmosphere of loving kindness' makes her weep, and she is also horrified to find herself tatting as a family quarrel rages around her, Betty returns on time to the sanatorium with her pulse and temperature perfectly normal but feeling very tired. She is worried that her family won't understand the concept of rest and quiet and staying up for only eight hours each day, the regimen she will have to maintain for some while if released. She looks healthier than any of them and much stronger than she actually is; although well on the road to recovery, she feels bewildered and unhappy.

Release

Those who successfully proved that their tuberculosis was arrested and that they had regained their strength were ready for discharge, again at the discretion of the Medical Director. Patients leaving Firland were instructed to continue getting as much rest as possible, to return regularly to the Firland Clinic for check-ups, to consult with their doctor when considering what type of employment to take up, and to remain alert to the reappearance of any tuberculosis symptoms. Women were advised against becoming pregnant. Both the Firland regime and these later strictures seemed to work: the National Tuberculosis Association found that Firland had a higher incidence of patients living a normal life five years following discharge than any other sanatorium in the country.

Discharges were announced on Mondays directly after rest hours and were given only to patients with eight or more hours up (except in the rare cases of those sent home to die). In *Plague* Betty comments that because nothing is ever revealed to patients about their progress, those in the eight-hours-and-more-up category never have any idea whether they might be nearing discharge and spend Monday rest hours rigid with hope. The lucky patients who do receive a discharge get an ovation at their next meal in the dining-room, while the others droop with disappointment and resign themselves to yet more time as an inmate.

It was very unusual to be discharged in under a year and although by June 1939 she is feeling quite well, in *Plague* Betty more or less gives up hope as Monday follows Monday. Her longing for home is so overwhelming that in spirit she has already left.

Then it happens. The Director tells her that her sputum has been negative since October and that she is in fine condition and can go home at once, but that she will have to continue pneumothorax for three to five years. Betty has made an unusually rapid and impressive recovery from a cavity in her left lung and a shadow on the right. She is no longer contagious and can be with her children.

Betty tries to thank him but the Director brushes it aside. Dr. Stith was personally responsible for all the admissions and discharges and ruled the sanatorium and the patients with a rod of iron, Betty wrote later. He would always say that people with tuberculosis were ungrateful, stupid, uncooperative, and unworthy. But at the same time he would accept no money from those who could not afford to pay and would buy bathrobes and pajamas for his uncooperative and stupid patients, take care of their families, listen to their problems and help them get work after their discharge. He shakes Betty by the hand and tells her to take care of herself.

Betty's happiness was so intense that she simply glowed, her fellow patient Monica Sone was to note in her own memoir. Betty herself wrote that on reaching home, and climbing into bed in a back room that no-one had gotten around to cleaning, she was happier than she had ever been in her life.

In *Plague* it takes Betty a long time to feel normal again. She had adjusted to the regimen in Firland and now she has to readjust to real life. The prison pallor disappears fairly quickly (although the scars of her surgeries are never to fade). Other marks of sanatorium life need concentrated effort to erase. At first she awakes early every day at about the time she had been awoken at Firland; making a pot of deliciously strong coffee she luxuriates over the morning paper until the others get up around seven. After about a month, though, she can wake up, realize she's at home, and be able to go back to sleep. She still needs to follow Firland's explicit instructions for care at home, which include frequent checks with her doctor; sleeping at least nine hours every night and taking a two-hour rest period during the day; sleeping in a bed alone, preferably in a room alone; and engaging in only moderate recreation and entertainment. If she doesn't play the game according to these rules there is the possibility of relapse.

In *Plague* Betty at first has no inclination to resume old friendships, preferring to maintain close contact with other discharged patients like 'Kimi' (Monica), who has also been discharged and comes to the house for lunch. Together they take frequent walks in the park discussing Firland. Betty knows she is going through an adjustment period but feels 'big and fat and whiny'.

One way to come to terms with the whole experience was to write about it. When Blanche dropped by at the house to welcome Betty back to the real world she found her friend perched on the built-in bench in the breakfast nook, pounding away on an old L.C. Smith typewriter. Casually dressed in frayed white pants, tattered white sweatshirt and tennis shoes spotted with paint, Betty was completely absorbed. Stacks of typewritten sheets covered the table. Betty laughingly told Blanche she was writing a book about her experiences at Firland, which she said she could never forget. She had kept a simple diary at Firland and her manuscript was in the same format. She later submitted the resulting work, entitled *In Bed We Laughed*, for the Atlantic Prize awarded by Atlantic Monthly Press, but received a rejection.

In *Plague* Betty is nervous on going for her first pneumothorax after her discharge but the doctor tells her she is in fine condition and can now stay up for twelve hours a day. Spells of depression continue, however, as does the tendency to huddle with her former fellow patients rather than re-enter the normal world. 'Kimi' still comes to the house almost every day and Betty confides to her friend her spells of black depression and her new obsession with housework, and how she bores Anne and Joan with too much attention and unskilled participation in their play. Added to her problems is the attitude of some people towards Betty as a former tuberculosis patient; many assume she is still contagious. Betty secretly dreads looking for a job and is worried that people in offices will react in the same way. Other people are kind and invite her round, but react with screams when they see her, telling her she looks ten years younger 'BUT SO MUCH FATTER!'

While at Firland, Betty had resigned her post at the US Treasury Department once her accrued sick leave and annual leave had run out, but now she was able to return to government service. She found a post at the National Youth Administration (a division of the Works Progress Administration where she had worked before) and remained there for the next three years. She appears to have totally regained her health, including feeling well enough to resume her heavy smoking habit, although she underwent intrapleural pneumolysis and pneumothorax as an outpatient for six further years, until the spring of 1945. She wrote later that when Firland's Medical Director Dr. Stith accepted her as a non-paying patient at the sanatorium he had told her that one day, when she had money, she could pay for someone else to get well. Incredibly, given that Betty was so poor at the time, she did end up making money when she became a best-selling author. There can be little doubt that giving to Firland was exactly what she did.

When *The Plague and I* was published in 1948 it was dedicated to Dr. Stith.

Betty and the Island

THE NATIONAL YOUTH ADMINISTRATION where Betty had found a job was another New Deal agency set up to provide work and education for young people. The Depression had brought special hardship to young Americans, preventing many from finishing school or entering the labor market, and denying them the opportunity to attain or improve skills. The NYA was a pet project of President Roosevelt's wife Eleanor, who had greatly feared losing the younger generation through lack of education and unemployment. Some 2.8 million young people were on relief in the mid 1930s and the organization was dedicated to helping those between the ages of sixteen and twenty-five either to stay in school or to obtain training and work experience. There were two streams at the NYA: the student work program enabling young people to remain in school or college, and the out-of-school employment program for those over sixteen. Participants in the programs received on-the-job training in construction, metal and woodworking, office work, recreation, and health care. Young NYA workers also performed useful work in parks, national forests, and other outdoor recreational areas.

Betty had a variety of tasks at the NYA and was ultimately appointed head of its Division of Information in Seattle. She seems to have loved what she did there: working on brochures, publicity releases and in-house magazines, and teaching the young people writing skills – an outlet at last for her own talent in this direction. She also supervised the production of signs and posters and other artwork. At any one time, Betty had between forty and ninety-five youth workers to supervise on projects as various as silkscreen printing and Youth Orchestra try-outs (during which she met, and cooked lunch for, conductor Leopold Stokowski). The next three years, until the NYA was eventually dissolved in 1943, were happy ones for Betty.

It was during this period that Betty met the well-known painter William Cumming through her friendship with the writer and journalist Margaret Bundy Callahan, family friend of the Bards and the former editor of *Town Crier* magazine which had published Betty's short story in 1933. Margaret was at the center of a coterie of artists and writers and it was at Margaret's one evening that Betty was introduced to Bill Cumming. Bill was a member of what became known as the Northwest School, painters interested in exploring the light and color of the Puget Sound area with an aesthetic much influenced by Japanese art. He was a significant voice in the development of the School, which was the first widely recognized artistic movement of the region. Always an eccentric, Bill would later call himself the 'Willie Nelson of Northwest Painting'. He too had written for the *Town Crier* and had a way with words. In the inimitable style of his memoir he gives us a very vivid portrait of Betty at this stage of her life:

One Callahan evening in particular was rendered riotous by the febrile chatter and staccato laugh of a frenetic young woman whose hair stands in memory as being on fire, a manifest absurdity occasioned by its hue of reddish gold. Beneath her hair her face played madly, the face of a gleeful fox. Round sallow cheeks set with greenish shadow sloped sharp to a pointy chin, her muzzle slit by a smallish mouth with a hint of asymmetric cupid's bow, prominent teeth bared in perpetual laughter setting off blue-green (or were they green?) eyes sparkling with unremitting malice towards the follies and witlessness of the race.

Bill described Betty keeping the party roaring with her oft-told stories of life as a chicken farmer, her voice 'crackling with excitement' as each story culminated in gales of wild, infectious laughter. Bill felt that Betty's humor wasn't kindly or homey or even friendly. 'It had the malicious edge of a scalpel, and it could cut,' was his verdict. Betty saw the deep flaws of the human race all too clearly, Bill believed, and she turned her acid humor on the stupidities of mankind because they enraged her. In his opinion her humor was also a deadly serious shield against a world which frightened her, although he described her sandpaper laugh as always joyous as she tore into pomposity and ignorance.

There are few contemporary descriptions of Betty and our view of her is for the most part informed by her own writing. Bill's depiction of her as manic and malicious is startling, to say the least. These are not qualities that emerge through her autobiographical writing, where the self she describes (retrospectively) is kinder, milder, more diffident. By this time of course Betty had survived an abusive marriage, hard times in the Depression and a brush with a fatal illness. She was no longer a shy young woman existing in her sister's shadow, but a maturing personality in her own right. A somewhat later pen portrait by *Cosmopolitan* magazine in 1947 suggested a similar propensity to rage, mentioning Betty's rapid shifts of expression from amusement to anger and the blazing of her eyes when talking about someone she disliked. (The same article described Betty as an able mimic, becoming in the space of half-an-hour a Swedish-American, a

Japanese-American, a vulgar Hollywood writer, an uppity female expert on foreign affairs and a bubbling Texas girl.)

When he first met Betty, Bill Cumming was working as a photographer and sketcher for the Federal Art Project, another part of the Works Progress Administration recovery program. Bill lost this employment in 1940 and his mentor Margaret Callahan suggested that perhaps he could work for Betty, who according to his memoir had just got her appointment as head of the NYA Division of Information. Betty would have been happy to take him on as her assistant but the budget did not allow for one, and so Bill had to join as a regular youth worker at $25 a month. Once enrolled he found he had no actual duties, so Betty suggested he paint pictures from the many sketches he had made of youth workers engaged on the various projects. This he did, but the pictures came to the attention of what Bill called the 'political hacks' in charge of the youth programs; these individuals then reportedly accused Betty of using the program to produce propaganda for 'subversion and overthrow of established law and order'. According to Bill this threw Betty into a furious rage in which she lost all sense of humor and threatened to walk out if Bill were dismissed. His version of events has Betty storming out of a meeting, still screaming, and leaving the cowed bureaucrats huddled mutely around the table before sheepishly approving a motion to keep Bill on. However, Bill also seems to say that he was not actually present at the meeting himself, so the veracity of his account may be in doubt. He carried on painting his pictures, helping Betty with paperwork which he said neither of them understood (an unlikely statement in Betty's case) and watching idly as she typed up the manuscript of *The Egg and I*.

This is not the only mention of Betty working on her writing while at the NYA. Another member of her staff recalled helping her type out what was to become *The Plague and I* during the lunch hour, and in 1978 the former State Head of the NYA himself claimed that Betty had told him that she had 'incubated' *Egg* while working at the agency. Betty appears to have stretched the truth a little when she wrote later that she only created *Egg* after Mary unexpectedly made an appointment for her with a publisher's agent.

Somewhere around 1940 Betty underwent an operation for the removal of ovarian cysts or polyps. Visiting her in hospital, Bill gave her an enormous brush and ink drawing of a brown bear. She lay in her bed looking a bit wasted after her surgery, her 'fox face sharpened to a point', laughing as he pinned the drawing up for her. But Betty did not return the courtesy of Bill's visit when he, like Betty, was stricken with TB and consigned to Firland. Betty accompanied him there for his first admittance in April 1942, repeating some of the funny stories she had already told him about the place and trying to buoy him up, but although she promised to visit she never showed. Bill eventually understood why, once he was discharged: he realized that old hands never liked to go back, even for a visit, in case they never got out again.

In 1941 the Japanese bombed Pearl Harbor in Hawaii. The attack came as a profound shock to Americans and led directly to the US entry into World War II. Betty called her close Japanese friend from the sanatorium, Monica Sone, to assure her that the war made no difference to their relationship. The NYA Information Division in Seattle was moved to a huge loft building at Twelfth and Madison and ordered to begin preparing for war by printing silkscreen armbands for Civilian Defense workers. A number of young Japanese Americans were transferred to the project, apparently in the belief that after Pearl Harbor they might be liable to attack from the populace and would be safer if engaged on defense work. Luckily no such attacks ever came, at least for the workers assigned to Betty's department. The young people made an efficient job of producing the armbands under what Bill called his and Betty's 'silly guardianship'. Betty's grasp was no doubt greater than Bill appreciated.

The mass internment of Japanese Americans ordered by President Roosevelt began in 1942. Monica's family were eventually among their number and before they were taken away, Monica asked Betty to look after a valuable Japanese doll: she knew Betty loved and appreciated beautiful things and that the doll would be safe, and enjoyed, in her keeping. During the Sones' internment Betty stayed in touch. When Monica sent her a letter begging her to send galoshes badly needed by the family to wade through their muddy camp, Betty combed Seattle and did everything she could to track some down for her old friend.

Don

Sometime around 1941 Betty met, or perhaps re-met, the slightly younger and darkly handsome Donald Chauncey MacDonald. Blanche described him as tall and round-faced with dark, close-cropped curls. With a name like that, Don was naturally of Scottish extraction – both parents were MacDonalds and his paternal grandfather came from Scotland. Don was born in 1910 in Council Bluffs, Iowa, one of at least nine children his father had sired by two wives; Don was among the second brood produced by his mother Beulah, who was much younger than his father. By the age of nine the family had moved to Douglas, Nebraska, and later ended up in Seattle. In *Onions in the Stew*, her book about this period in her life, Betty wrote that Don came from a Free Methodist family and by his own account had had a pretty austere upbringing – hauling ashes to earn money for school clothes and enduring hours of praying in church on bony knees. Even allowing for Betty's usual comic exaggeration, Don probably did have a hard childhood. His father Clinton worked as a carpenter when in Nebraska and later as a gardener, providing for his large family on whatever he was able to earn by this hard manual work.

Don and Betty's lives had followed remarkably similar paths. Just as in Betty's childhood, Don's family had moved around during his early years. Like Betty, he attended both Roosevelt High School and the University of Washington, where he studied Economics and Business. He worked in the burglar alarm industry before starting at the university in his late twenties and, again like Betty, he did not graduate, attending only for the year 1938-39. In 1940 at the age of twenty-nine he was still living with his family at home, just as Betty had done for so many years, and was again employed in the burglar alarm business. In *Onions* and other writing Betty portrayed Don, affectionately, as taciturn and given to quoting grim Scots poetry at every setback. He was certainly averse to frivolous chat – Blanche described Don excusing himself to go and get a cup of coffee, or returning to his car, whenever she and Betty met by chance and were exchanging their usual stories.

Betty's marriage to her 'dour Scotsman', as she called him, took place in April 1942. She was thirty-five and Don was thirty-one. Betty's sister Alison and her fiancé were witnesses at the wedding, which took place thirty miles north of Seattle in Everett, Snohomish County – possibly because Betty wanted to avoid applying for a wedding license in Seattle where she was known. At that time it was illegal in Washington State for any woman under the age of forty-five with advanced pulmonary tuberculosis to marry, and although Betty's disease had never been advanced, nevertheless discretion may have seemed advisable.

Don was not Betty's first serious relationship since her marriage to Bob: there are references in her correspondence to at least one failed romance. But she appears to have fallen hard for Don, and their decision to marry was made quickly. In later life Anne recalled that the first she even heard of Don was when she came upon him sitting with Betty in the breakfast nook in the kitchen, Betty wearing an orchid on her lapel to celebrate. She introduced Don to Anne as her new Daddy. Both the girls used the surname MacDonald soon after their mother's marriage, and were later formally adopted by Don (they thought Don 'very handsome', Blanche recalled.)

Don was by then a defense worker engaged in the final testing of aircraft produced at Boeing's Renton plant in Seattle. (In August that year the *Seattle Times* reported that Boeing electrician Donald C. MacDonald, possibly Don, had been denied new tires to which he was entitled as a defense worker because of 'abuse of rubber' through speeding. The rationing board decreed that he could not buy new tires until the war was over.)

Betty was not the only Bard sister to marry that year. Alison tied the knot in June with musician and composer Frank Sugia. Theirs was a classic white wedding complete with white satin and lace dress, Anne as one of the bridesmaids and Mary's two little daughters as flower girls. Dede, aged twenty-eight, followed suit in 1943 with Navy man Melvin Goldsmith. All the Bard sisters were now married.

Mike Gordon was still sending his extravagant gifts to Betty and the family and in her subsequent article about Mike for *Reader's Digest* Betty wrote that she thought, with relief, that with her marriage to Don the torrent of gifts would at last cease. On the contrary, the article went on, Mike and Don met and formed a mutual admiration society. Don thought Mike was amazing, funny and sweet. Mike dubbed Don a handsome fellow and a 'Scotchman just like me'. The presents continued but in a new, masculine form. Little motors, fifty gallons of anti-freeze and cases of whiskey arrived along with the usual mounds of seasonal fruit for the children. Mike appeared to be courting Don as well as Betty, and Don then had to join Betty in the business of trying to find gifts for Mike that weren't immediately topped by something several times as expensive coming straight back. It was a problem that couldn't be solved, Betty wrote – until much later when she produced the best-selling *The Egg and I* and herself became 'wealty and prrrominent'. This turned out to be the ultimate payback as it gave Mike the opportunity to carry round dozens of copies of the book in his car and toss them to all his friends, telling them it was the biggest thing since the Bible. He died in 1947, and Betty attended the lavish funeral to deliver a eulogy – unusually for her as she disapproved of funerals. Don was an honorary pallbearer.

§

The Depression was over, and with the US now in the war the federal government needed planes and ships. The State of Washington could build both. Roosevelt's public works projects to create employment during the 1930s had included the building of the Bonneville Dam on the Columbia River, and this along with other Columbia River dams was able to power the shipyards of Vancouver and Puget Sound. The same cheap energy also made Seattle into one of the nation's aircraft capitals, as electricity-powered aluminum plants could supply Boeing with the material needed to build America's bomber squadrons. By the end of 1942, 150,000 workers were laboring around the clock in the state's shipyards and aircraft factories – including the first ever 'girl welders' at Boeing. After the bitter times of the previous decade Washington State was succeeding at a new economy, one which only federal investment during the Depression had made possible. But with this burgeoning wartime growth, workers had flooded in to Seattle, and there was little accommodation to be had. As a new family Betty and Don, plus Anne and Joan, needed to find somewhere of their own. Up until her remarriage Betty was still living at home, in the same shingled house, with the girls, her mother, one sister and honorary sister Madge.

In Betty's account in *Onions in the Stew*, Don is living in a dark apartment just off the campus of the University of Washington and when his room-mate moves out, Don and Betty spend their weekend honeymoon (all that was allowed defense workers) right there in the apartment. Betty then moves in, with the girls for the moment remaining at Sydney's. A notice of eviction then arrives from the landlord giving them about one week to leave. For a brief period they live in the apartment above, but the noise in the neighborhood in the warmer months means that shift-worker Don can get no sleep. Betty starts house-hunting but in Seattle there are no houses available to rent and none on sale for the kind of money Betty and Don have, which is pretty much nothing. Looking further afield, and after extensive searches on nearby Bainbridge and Whidbey Islands, they finally track down the perfect place on Vashon, a 15-mile-long island just across from Seattle in Puget Sound and accessible only by ferry-boat. The owners keep changing their minds about selling but after a summer of vacillation the move finally takes place in October 1942.

By now Betty's honorary sister Madge was also married, the last to go, and so Sydney moved in with Mary and the old house on 15th Avenue was rented out. Mary's husband Clyde was overseas in the Navy, and Sydney helped care for their three children while Mary was busy running Clyde's pathology laboratory and volunteering at an officers' canteen. In the end Sydney was to live more or less with Betty on the island; they got on well and were good friends.

Vashon

Beautiful Vashon is superbly described in *Onions*: the lushness, the spectacular views of Mount Rainier, the frequent harshness of a life cut off from the mainland. In 1942 when Betty and Don arrived, the population was still in the low 3,000s. Today, the population is well over ten thousand but the lack of a bridge from the mainland has meant that Vashon still retains the rustic character and sense of isolation that Betty knew. It's home to many artists, writers, musicians and organic farmers. The orchards and strawberry farms of Betty's time no longer play a major role in the island's economy but Vashon continues to hold its annual strawberry festival, and is now called Vashon-Maury Island because of the isthmus connecting it with the neighboring island of that name.

The year the MacDonalds arrived the island was much affected, as everywhere else in the country, by the continuing war. Air raid drills were being held and volunteer-staffed air raid observation posts had been set up; there was training in the High School on medical care and how to black out the home; there were scrap iron and copper drives. Tires, fuel, and coffee were all rationed. On 16 May the order had been issued for the evacuation of the island's Japanese American residents and 126 had been taken away, despite the fact that other of Vashon's Japanese Americans had already volunteered to defend their country and were serving in US forces. Vashon had to prepare itself for possible invasion by Japan, and at the time the US authorities viewed all Japanese American people as potential fifth columnists. The population of the island had been decimated in other ways. Many had left to work at Boeing, including even some teachers and school principals, because there was more money to be earned there. In June of 1942 strawberry pickers were in short supply because many of the usual workers were in defense jobs or the military, and efforts were made to attract Native American pickers in their stead.

Betty and Don's new place on Vashon, bought without a down payment, was literally a house on the beach, a hand-built cabin in seven acres located about a quarter of a mile south of Dolphin Point to the east side of the island. The walls of the house were built of hewn fir, the floor planks came from old ship decking, the roof was made of hand-split cedar shakes (shingles made from split logs) and the rain and salt air had turned it all a soft silvery gray. Directly below the house stretched the log-strewn beach. Inside, Betty placed yellow pots of red geraniums on the window sills of the cheerful kitchen, which was separated from the large living room by a dining area. From the living room a few steps led up to a little balcony onto which opened three bedrooms and a bathroom; the thin, highly polished log railings running along the balcony and the hand-hewn rafters on the high ceiling gave the house an old-fashioned rustic air. Mount Rainier could be glimpsed from the windows.

But although charming, the house was built originally as a summer home and during the colder months was freezing. The cavernous granite fireplace demanded mountains of wood and when Betty first started to write books she often had to type in the cold, wearing gloves with the fingertips cut off. Blanche said it was a dramatic place, very beachy-looking, but that she was never quite warm enough when she visited.

The only way to reach the house was by the mile-and-a-half walking trail from the ferry or by landing a boat on the beach. In *Onions in the Stew*, kindly new neighbors allow them to use their private road to get part-way to the beach and also give them the use of some boats. Don and a friend helping with the move tie the boats together and load up everything they have, including the washing machine, to bring in by water. This really was how they moved in, according to an interview Anne and Joan gave many years later.

The girls were soon enrolled at local schools on the island, Joan in seventh grade at the Vashon grade school, Anne as freshman in Vashon High School. For Betty and Don, everyday life was now complicated not only by war conditions on the island but also by the necessary commute by ferry to the mainland for their jobs. In *Onions* Betty, by taking shortened lunch hours, is allowed to arrive in the morning at eight instead of wartime seven-thirty. Don has finished his night shifts but has to be at Boeing's Renton plant by six-thirty in the morning, and so catches the five-fifteen ferry. Each morning they get up at four-thirty (a painful reminder to Betty of other early starts as the wife of a chicken farmer), warm up the kitchen by turning the oven on, and eat the breakfast Betty has laid out the night before. Then Don shoots out of the door into the rain and darkness, allowing himself sixteen minutes to run up the beach (if the tide's out), start the car, and drive the mile and a half to the ferry.

At five-thirty Betty gets the girls' breakfast and then takes a shower in the cold, dark little service-room downstairs, having first checked for slugs and spiders. After waking the girls at six-thirty and refereeing their quarrels, Betty then has to leave them to get themselves to school while she sets off before seven to catch the seven-twenty ferry. She wears sensible shoes and socks over her silk stockings, carries her office shoes, and usually has to run the last quarter mile of the trail to the dock to get there in time for the ferry. The trail stretched from the house to the dock along the steep southeast face of the island about fifty feet above the shore; in the spring and summer it's overgrown with nettles and in the fall it's slippery and cobwebby. Occasionally, after a storm, the trail might slide off the hill altogether and Betty would have to pick her uncertain way across the face of a seeping bank. At a certain point she can see whether the ferry is coming in, is in already, or is going out again, and she starts running accordingly. By the time she gets to work she's boiling hot and then has to sit for the rest of the day in an office which is heated to 80 degrees, filled with smoke, and has the windows firmly shut. That her only recently healed lungs could cope with this regime defies belief.

Vashon was a beautiful place to live but conditions could be harsh. The elements were hardly kind: rain, heat, cold, earthquakes, snow, mountain slides, storms, fog and wind could all be extreme. In *Onions* getting wood for the fire dominates the family's existence whatever the weather. The fireplace in the living room is enormous and can accommodate several huge logs. At first going for wood seems like fun – all they have to do is go down to the beach and pick up bark brought by the tide, or go up to the woods behind the house and roll it down. There is fir and alder and cedar and to start with, in the fall, they keep huge fires burning from early morning till late at night. Then the days begin getting shorter, the bark tides fewer and the days wetter and colder. There is considerably less enthusiasm about fetching wood and the family take to wearing extra clothing and letting the animals sleep on the couches and chairs to keep them warm. It was like living in a mine, Betty wrote: dark and damp and cold the whole day, whether getting up or going to bed.

On the other hand, the island offered abundant sources of food to make up for wartime shortages. The MacDonalds' private beach offered clams, geoducks, sea cucumbers, squid, crabs, piddocks, cockles and mussels. By going out in the rowing boat they could catch sole, salmon, cod, Spanish mackerel, red snapper and perch. Other edibles available on their property were blackberries, huckleberries, watercress, and mushrooms, although Betty was wary about the mushrooms after suffering an episode of poisoning. Vegetation on the island grew madly and a neighbor in later years remembered Don driving down their shared road with the car door open, machete in hand as he hacked back the weeds.

Reading between the lines of *Onions in the Stew*, Betty was now really enjoying life after so many bad experiences; the past was behind her. Her marriage was happy, and, in *Onions* at least, the girls had readily accepted Don as their stepfather. She and Don were only in their early thirties and finally had just enough money, although Betty remarks caustically that any man not down on all fours is automatically paid twice as much as the brightest woman. They were living in a very picturesque spot, even if it was mostly freezing and they were often at the mercy of the elements. In the book Betty writes happily about the joys of digging clams on their own beach; the riotous growth of anything and everything they plant in the garden; their hardy and sometimes eccentric island neighbors; the raccoons who come right up the house to eat the family's leftovers and the candy Betty buys just for them; and the constant stream of guests in the summer, usually Mary accompanied by several friends. While her husband was away on war service Mary wasn't sitting around: she was engaged in a number of worthwhile causes and did plenty of entertaining, which tended to include Betty's lovely place on Vashon, usually without much notice. On one occasion, according to Blanche, she arrived with several guests in tow only to be greeted by an unpleasant odor: the septic tank was backed up. Mary simply declared that it was the ultimate in hospitality for a hostess to clean out the septic tanks for her guests, and sailed on in.

There's a whole chapter on the family's cats and dogs that Betty loved so much; she could never quite like anyone who didn't like dogs, she once wrote. Another chapter, on food, is mostly about other people's bad cooking and has plenty of acerbic comments about the type of revolting lima bean, jelly and macaroni casserole 'so dear to the heart of the bum cook'. Loving children and animals and cooking good food were at the heart of Betty's love of home; she was invariably happiest on the domestic scene. She still loved to paint, and would turn out tempera landscapes and pastels of the children. Despite her successful career in government service, and her subsequent worldwide fame as a writer, she often talked about wanting to stay home and do homey things like painting porch furniture rather than go out to work. 'I am first, last and always a wife and mother,' she once firmly declared.

There was, of course, the occasional fly in the ointment. In *Onions* 'Lesley Arnold' is a glamorous woman living on Vashon who appears to be making a dead set at Don:

Lesley Arnold's voice was husky to that fascinating point just short of asthma...so beautiful she made me slightly sick at my stomach...She made me feel just like a hygiene teacher.

A hot hygiene teacher in an ugly tan knitted suit, the wrong shoes and no husband. Don, my honest, blunt Scotsman, was so dashing (drooling?) that even the girls were impressed.

'Lesley', whose Navy husband is mostly absent, keeps inveigling Don into her house with spurious jobs that require a man. Don likes Lesley and the girls adore her and they all make Betty feel like a pariah if she ventures even the slightest criticism.

This glamorous rival for Don's affections was based in reality. One evening Blanche, who had also ended up living on the island, was at the MacDonalds' for dinner. It got later and later and still Don hadn't arrived home; Betty knew where he was, and started to become upset. Sydney was present too and Betty asked her mother whether she should call the woman's house, but Sydney advised against it. She told Betty to go and tidy herself up, put on fresh clothes and comb her hair. 'Lesley' no doubt looked very alluring and was turning on the charm, she told her anxious daughter, and if Don came home and found Betty tired, mad, and sarcastic, the contrast would not be in her favor. Betty followed this advice and when Don finally strolled up the path she was cheerful, looked lovely and did not mention how late he was. That evening she served up a succulent beef roast in pastry, fluffy mashed potatoes with gravy, and a side salad of avocado and grapefruit. The Bards disliked sweet things, and dessert was just grapes and an assortment of cheeses. She received compliments from Don, and in Blanche's opinion won the contest with 'Lesley' hands down. In *Onions in the Stew* this rival eventually moves away, and Betty wrote that she and Don were both relieved. (There was another potential rival mentioned in *Onions in the Stew* with whom Don on one occasion shares a blanket on board the deck of a yacht. Don may or may not have had a roving eye, but

Betty always maintained, at least in public, that they were very happily married.)

Betty and Blanche were able to renew their old friendship once they discovered that each had moved, unbeknownst to the other, to Vashon. They were soon cracking their old jokes and having fun together. Blanche was forever amazed and amused by her friend's verbal quickness. Once she and Betty were talking about some offbeat people they knew who had rather peculiar sleeping arrangements within the family. Blanche remembered Betty saying, 'Of course they 'incested' everything was open and above board.' On another occasion both were at a PTA meeting at Joan's school in Vashon where Blanche worked as a teacher. They were sitting together, something Blanche knew was a mistake because Betty's remarks always cracked her up. Immediately they were giggling at the contrast presented by the formally dressed, begloved and behatted PTA president and the casually dressed islanders. The president presented a gift to the school's large and forthright cook: a record of Rimsky-Korsakov's *Scheherazade Suite.* The cook wrinkled her brow and asked, 'The *what* suite?' Betty whispered to Blanche that she'd rather have had *Yes! We Have No Bananas* and Blanche collapsed. Another time Blanche was buying an item at the Vashon hardware store but, discovering she had left her handbag behind, asked if she could pay for the item the following day. Then she heard a voice from the store entrance – Betty, deliberately dropping consonants as she called out, 'There's that deadbeat of a Mrs. Hutchin's, trying to get out of paying for stuff again. Ha, saying she's forgotten her purse.' Blanche got her own back by loudly accusing Betty and Don of hoarding coffee when they came to pick up their ration stamps.

Life on Vashon proved so beguiling that Betty's siblings began to move to the island too. In 1943, one year after Betty and Don had bought their place, Alison, her husband and infant son Darsie took up residence in a big old house within easy reach of her big sister. Betty and Alison had had different interests growing up but now they grew closer and became good friends, despite a possible element of jealousy in the relationship. (When Alison sadly gave birth to a stillborn daughter, Betty in private correspondence talked of Sydney's deep grief and remarked that her mother was 'worshipping' at the shrine of Alison.) However, once Alison was living on the island, Betty often took care of Alison's small children when her sister was busy working as a fashion model for a large Seattle department store.

Cleve too ended up on Vashon, buying a small old house likewise within easy reach of Betty's. Cleve as an adult was tall, rugged and red-haired, and according to Blanche, looked like photographs of his father Darsie. He became active in civic affairs on Vashon and ran a successful construction business. Mary moved to Vashon also, albeit many years later.

Being closer together made it even easier for the family to continue all their old traditions. Hosting Christmas was always shared between the sisters. One or other of them would hold the main gathering on Christmas Eve, offering ham, turkey and a flaming plum pudding, and after the feast the assembled mass of excited children would gather to hear Sydney read traditional Christmas tales aloud. At around ten, when any guests in for the evening had taken their departure and the children had been persuaded into bed, the adults in the family would set about opening their Christmas presents. On Christmas

Day they would all gather again at the home of another sister.

The remaining years of the war grew ever more difficult. In 1943 shoes and meat were rationed; new War Loan and paper drives helped the war effort. Army Fighter Command moved onto the island and took charge of the air raid observation posts. Some on the island called for the return of the Japanese American residents now interned in camps on the mainland; others opposed it. Harvesting Vashon's abundant fruit without sufficient manpower remained a problem, and in 1944 Native Americans from the Quinault people were given Victory Farm Worker badges for their work picking cherries, currants and loganberries at $10 – 12 a day.

Finally, in 1945, came victory. The war was over.

For the first few months Don continued the commute by ferry to his work on the mainland. Betty was doing a variety of jobs. Then, without warning, life changed in a way they could never have foreseen.

The Egg and I

In February 1943, Betty was working for a Government contractor in Seattle and making good money. Then, according to her account in *Anybody Can Do Anything*, an old friend of Mary's arrives in the city and announces that he is a talent scout for a publishing firm. He's looking for Northwest authors so Mary, of course, says that her sister Betty is a writer but that she doesn't know how much Betty has done on her book. According to Betty she has done so little she hasn't even thought of writing one. Mary then calls Betty at work in Seattle only a quarter of an hour before an appointment she's made for her with the scout (Blanche's memory, on the other hand, was that Betty had her hands in the dishwasher at home on Vashon when Mary's call came through). Walking to the appointment Betty decides to produce a refutation of the then popular life-is-wonderful books by the wives of men who have forced them to live in the country and draw up all their water from a well – a reference to works such as Louise Dickinson Rich's 1942 book *We Took to the Woods*, an enthusiastic account of living and raising a family in the backwoods of Maine which Joan remembered her mother reading. The publisher's representative likes the idea and asks her to write a five-thousand-word outline for the following night.

However, evidence shows that in fact Betty had attempted to write about both her life with the chickens and her stay in Firland well before the appearance of any talent scout. She may well have had rough manuscripts in readiness, had perhaps even submitted them already to a publisher. But whatever the genesis of *Egg*, Betty had some very firm ideas about what she wanted to express. She once wrote to a fan:

> *The idea in writing the book was to furnish a rebuttal to such books as WE TOOK TO THE WOODS and LIVING HIGH and WILDERNESS WIFE. I enjoyed the books but got damned tired of hearing the pioneer life pictured as the ideal existence for a woman. I have always maintained that those books were actually written as a justification for the husband's queer choice of occupations. To me, a woman who says that she prefers to live without lights, water, telephone or friends, is on a par with a person who says that he enjoys having athlete's foot.*

Betty has never before written anything like an outline, or a book, her narrative continues in *Anybody Can Do Anything* (despite the evidence to the contrary). It's slow going and she needs to stay home from work the next day to finish it. She asks a friend at the office to say she's sick but for some reason the friend tells her boss the truth and Betty is fired.

The publisher's representative, who was the West Coast editor for Doubleday, Doran and Company, told Betty to send the outline in to Doubleday and to proceed with the book. She did so, followed in due course by the first chapters of *Egg*, written in diary form, and one of the *Mrs. Piggle-Wiggle* stories she used to tell the girls. But time went on without hearing anything further and Betty was forced to find work. Eventually that particular editor left the company and sent Betty's manuscripts back, at which point all work on *Egg* languished until Mary began to prod. 'Are you going to spend all your life washing your sheets by hand, or are you going to make $50,000 a year writing?' she asked her sister.

There then followed a long, long year as Betty struggled to produce *The Egg and I*, sometimes putting it away in disgust and getting boring little part-time jobs until Mary pushed her to pick it up again. Finally Betty started hand-painting greeting cards for a company. The job was to tint tiny little photographs of 'The Majesty of Mount Rainier' or 'Beautiful Lake Washington in the Sunset', using dabs of cotton dipped in paint (blue for the sky, green for trees, orange for sunsets, and pink for rhododendrons). The company would then take back the finished photographs and glue them onto cards bearing appropriate verses. Betty was paid one-and-a-half cents for Christmas cards and two-and-a-half cents for Easter and Mother's Day cards, which were slightly larger. If she ripped through her housework, did no writing and painted all day as she listened to soap operas on the radio, Betty could make as much as $41.76 a week. She really loved painting the cards and would have kept right on doing it, she wrote later in an article, but for Mary constantly calling to check if she was getting on with her writing. Mary would yell that Betty was a 'little-money-thinker' because she would rather have $41.76 than $50,000 from writing a best-seller, but Betty's reasoning was that $41.76 was a real sum that she could make every week, which was a whole lot better than a mythical sum of $50,000. But usually Mary's pushing was enough for her to get back to work on the book.

But with money still tight, in February 1944 Betty attempted, yet again, to extract some money from her ex-husband Bob Heskett. Over the past years the $30 a month mandated by the court had of course failed to materialize, and Bob now owed her the then huge sum of $4260. Through her attorney Betty presented an affidavit for a Writ of Garnishment – meaning a levy on earnings or possessions – against Bob's very much younger sister Dorothy, whom she believed to be holding some of Bob's possessions. Dorothy responded to the court that she was not holding any of Bob's things and that in fact she herself owed her brother a couple of hundred dollars. The court promptly ordered this money to be paid to Betty. There are no records to show whether Betty ever got either this or the full sum she was owed in support by Bob. By the following year it would hardly matter.

Despite what appears to have been the hard slog of writing it, in later years Betty was to observe that she was fresh and enthusiastic when she created *Egg* and that therefore it was her best book, even though she believed the writing was much better in *Onions in the Stew*. But whether it was hard going or written with enthusiasm, there was pain in reawakening memories of her marriage to Bob – she told a fan that in writing it she had relived the experiences 'to an uncomfortable degree' – as well as enjoyment in reversing the image of the game pioneer woman and poking fun at herself as the ultimate reluctant homesteader.

In February 1944, when the book was nearly finished, Betty set about trying to sell it again. She sent a detailed outline to the New York literary agents Brandt & Brandt, who had rejected some of her short stories in the past. She told them that she also had a draft of her book about her time as a tuberculosis patient and several *Mrs. Piggle-Wiggle* stories (one of which she had already submitted to other publishers). In her note to the agency Betty joked that the book should probably be called *We Don't Take to the Woods*, a reference again to the more positive title of the back-to-nature tale written by Louise Dickinson Rich.

An editing agent at Brandt & Brandt, Bernice Baumgarten, asked to see the manuscript of *Egg* and liked it, although not convinced that it lived up to the outline. She suggested a narrative rather than a diary form, and more early biographical detail to pad out the too-short manuscript. Betty duly added in an account of her childhood in Butte, and stories of eccentric Gammy and the rest of her rambunctious family.

Bernice was also dubious about what she perceived as a bitter ending to the book: it seemed to her that Betty at one point almost hated Bob. Betty admitted that this might be so, responding that Bob was 'the most concentrate bastard that ever lived', but that she had hoped it was not obvious:

He was very handsome, very very attractive but I was definitely not the one to bring out the best in him. I tried, when writing about him, to keep my present husband, who is six foot two and very handsome and a lamb, before me but apparently I slipped.

She promised to fix this as she was not writing a True Confession – meaning not the real story of her life with Bob Heskett – although if she did, 'it would be a dilly'. Bob's character was duly smoothed out to appear more callous than cruel, even though the unhappiness of the marriage was still all too apparent.

Bernice Baumgarten sold *Egg* to publisher J. B. Lippincott on the basis of the outline alone. Bernice was more than happy with Betty's revised manuscript, and so was the publisher – although both had some reservations about the possibility of libel. The book was scheduled for immediate serialization in the respected *Atlantic Monthly* magazine and appeared in the June, July and August 1945 issues. (It would later be serialized in the equally respected *New Yorker*.) The book might well have ended up with a different title, but *Atlantic Monthly*'s press release announcing the serialization as *The Egg and I* scuppered Lippincott's last-minute notion to change it to *Fine Feathered Friends*. The first few copies rolled off the presses that July, well in advance of the planned October publication date.

Lippincott's salesman for the Pacific Coast took Betty to dinner and told her he thought the book was going to be a best-seller. Betty thought he was either trying to cheer her up or had been talking to her mother, who naturally believed it was going to be a best-seller because she was convinced everything her children did was superb. Betty herself didn't think it was going to be any kind of seller and had actually got in touch with the card-painting company to say that the book was finished and that she was again available. The manager of the company was very nice, and genuinely interested in the book, and advised her not to put her own picture on the jacket but to use a picture of a pretty girl in order to sell more copies.

Betty dedicated the book to Mary (later dubbed Betty's Boswell), 'who has always believed that I can do anything she puts her mind to.'

Betty and Fame

THE EGG AND I is a very funny, lightly fictionalized account of Betty's life on the chicken farm with Bob, (or a version of Bob). Although she said she wrote it 'because it was the last untamed frontier' she hardly portrays herself as a pioneer woman; instead, she points up the disconnect between the (then) accepted duties of a wife to support her husband's goals and learn to love what he does, and the hard realities of isolated farm life. The writing is colorful and immediate, and startlingly frank in parts for the 1940s. A well-known writer and critic of the time, Clifton Fadiman, observed drily that Betty called a spade a spade, and that there were plenty of spades. Her neighbors, the 'Kettles' in particular, are described without mercy, but inevitably Betty's own idiosyncratic family are painted far more affectionately, even the overbearing Mary. An undercurrent of sadness surfaces towards the end as Betty's marriage with Bob starts to disintegrate (although in line with the more conformist expectations of the time, no mention of their eventual divorce), but Betty's trademark humor and optimism never falter.

At the same time, a real sense of Betty's feeling for the beautiful Northwest is conveyed through her expressive writing.

...suddenly the windows in the kitchen would begin to lighten a little and I knew it was time for the sunrise. I'd rush outdoors just as the first little rivulets of pale pink began creeping shyly over the mountains. These became bolder and brighter until the colors were leaping and

cascading down the mountains and pouring into the pond at the foot of the orchard. Faster and faster they came until there was a terrific explosion of color and the sun stood on the top of the mountains laughing at us.

She mourns the depredations made by the logging companies, the only ugliness she ever saw. Whole mountains were left scarred, she wrote, and lovely lakes turned muddy brown with woody debris and rubbish.

Before *The Egg and I* was finally published the family would sit around the fire at night in their beach house on Vashon, trying to keep warm and discussing what they would do with the money if 'The Book' sold two hundred copies, or maybe even four hundred. Betty wanted a fireplace in every room and a big wide road down to the house so the family would no longer have to walk the slippery narrow trail. Groceries could be delivered instead of having to carry them down the one-and-a-half miles by knapsack. Don wanted a case of imported Scotch, a case of Money's mushrooms (a high-quality supplier) and big locks for his closets so the girls couldn't borrow his clothes. But absolutely no road; Don preferred privacy. Like Betty, teenaged Anne and Joan wanted warmth and to have blast furnaces installed in every room of the big drafty house. They also clamored for a charge account at the Vashon Pharmacy so they could buy lipstick and nail polish when they wanted. And they *did* want the road.

Then things started to happen. Expectations at Lippincott were low, and little was done in the way of fanfare when the book first came out. But, in the immediate aftermath of World War II, Americans were weary and desperate for a return to happier times and something to laugh about; they greeted the irreverent humor and the absolute freshness of the book with delight. There was great appeal in a comic account of a life lived close to the earth, in not so distant times, when life had been simpler. At the same time the book may also have come as a relief to an increasingly urban population feeling uneasy about their soft life of air-conditioning and huge Frigidaires; they may have welcomed Betty's message that the simple life was not all it was made out to be. One New York reviewer commented: 'To city people sitting smug and dry, Mrs. MacDonald's life in the woods comes as unadulterated fun.'

Egg received rave reviews and, to the family's utter amazement, the book began flying off the shelves. Continuing wartime paper and cloth shortages meant that initial print runs were unable to meet the demand, and Lippincott were forced to put other titles from their fall 1945 list on the back burner. Soon after publication, Betty was told she had earned $25,000 in royalties in the space of just six days. By December, *Egg* had reached number one on the *New York Times* non-fiction best-seller list, a position it held for forty-three weeks. It was to remain in the top five for seven months and to dominate the *Publisher's Weekly* non-fiction best-seller lists for a period of three years.

Just before the money started rolling in, Betty, Don and Sydney went to have dinner with Blanche in her home on Vashon. Mary had insisted Betty buy a new dress to be famous in. For Betty, clothes were never a priority. Just give me a nice raincoat, some sweaters, pants, and a couple of skirts, and I'm all set, she would say. However, on this occasion she had bought a soft, black, sheer wool dress trimmed in leopard fur. The color suited her reddish-brown hair and gold-toned complexion perfectly, and Blanche thought she looked lovely. Mary had had to loan her the money, though, because at this particular point Betty was spending what little money she had on long-distance calls to her agent. But penny-pinching was soon to be a thing of the past. When the first check for $10,000 finally arrived from her publisher, Betty and her sister Alison immediately went to Kimmel's, the Vashon grocery store, to buy food for a celebration dinner. Eating good food was the way the Bards celebrated any happy event. For the first time Betty paid no attention to prices as they chose the best wine the store had to offer, a beautiful, fresh king salmon and three bags of expensive wild rice; Alison remembered the bill as being more than she usually paid for food in a month. Anne and Joan spent the celebration dinner making out lists of the clothes they wanted to buy and the outfits they had longed for.

Limelight

With the totally unexpected success of her book a dumbfounded Betty found herself sucked into a frenzy of publicizing, speaking engagements, radio, TV and book tours. In fact all of the family became instant celebrities. After *Egg* sold eight thousand copies in just one day, a *Life* photographer moved in with the family for a week and took hundreds of pictures of Betty and the girls, and publicity-shy Don when he could find him (nearly everyone confused Don with Bob Heskett, Betty's first husband who had featured so prominently in the book). The multi-page spread, *Life Goes Calling on the Author of The Egg and I*, appeared in March 1946. The article stated that *Egg* had sold 250,000 copies to date and had been the number one best-selling non-fiction book for ten weeks running and that Betty had earned $40,000 in less than a year (more than $500,000 today). Betty was described as a 'pretty and ebullient red-head of 37 who looks ten years younger', and was photographed in various staged situations: reading fan mail with the girls, sitting at her typewriter while surrounded by a crowd of children, and buying eggs in a Vashon store. Anne and Joan of course loved all the fun and excitement and were having a wonderful time.

Lippincott wanted Betty to meet the press more widely and that spring Betty and Don set off on a country-wide promotional tour, the first time that Betty had ever traveled east as an adult. Sydney accompanied them part of the way and Betty wrote Mary from Texas that their mother was simply wonderful to travel with – never tiring or complaining and always ready to eat and drink something. In the same letter Betty said she 'loathed' Southern California but loved Texas and found Texans charming, helpful and friendly. At this point so early in her fame Betty was clearly enjoying herself and was impressed by some of the fancy places they were staying in. During their first stop in Portland, Oregon, they stayed in an enormous suite with three bathrooms and she, Don and Sydney all took baths at the same time 'just to be rich'. From another hotel she wrote Mary on the hotel's stationery about their room with its 'red and white dotted swiss curtains and white chintz draperies with red roses'. Everyone in San Francisco was dressed so beautifully, she told Anne and Joan, that she felt like she was from Alaska.

Everywhere she went Betty was fêted, from a cocktail party in the Beverly Wilshire in Los Angeles to drinks with store owners in Dallas. Hotels were not booked everywhere for them en route and sometimes they had to find somewhere to stay at dead of night, but Betty assured Mary she was having a wonderful trip. After a grueling schedule taking in San Francisco, Los Angeles, Dallas, New Orleans, Atlanta and Baltimore, they finally arrived in New York in late February. *The Seattle Times* reported on her program:

Mrs. MacDonald will have a busy schedule when she arrives in Manhattan. She will be the guest of honor at the New York Herald Tribune Book and Author luncheon at the Hotel Astor March 5. Her publishers, J. B. Lippincott Co., will present her to New York literary celebrities at a cocktail party Wednesday, March 6 at the Ritz-Carlton. Tuesday, March 12 she will be in Washington, D.C. to be guest speaker at the Washington Post Book and Author luncheon at the Hotel Statler, and later in the month she will speak at the annual banquet of the Women's Book Association at the Hotel Pennsylvania. She will make four radio appearances.

Betty had bought a new wardrobe to wow them on the trip but found she hadn't always got it right. 'I bought a sheared beaver coat and thought it very elegant,' she told an interviewer that year, 'and then, when I got to New York, I discovered the only way to be exclusive was to own a cloth coat.' Nevertheless, normally shy Betty appears to have held her own. During the two-day promotion trip to Washington she talked to a sell-out crowd of 655 at the Book and Author luncheon and, according to the *Seattle Times*, won prolonged applause with her 'frank comments, infectious and frequent smiles, easy poise and off-hand wit'.

It was during probably this visit to New York that Betty was asked to speak at the Dutch Treat Club, a prestigious society for illustrators, writers and performers such as Robert Benchley and Ogden Nash. Because of her rapid rise to fame Betty was one of the first women guests to invade this stuffy male sanctum and she was terrified. On this particular day, to make matters worse, the other speaker was actually Winston Churchill, the former wartime Prime Minister of Great Britain. The famous statesman gallantly soothed Betty's shaking terror, and awe at meeting Churchill, by offering and sharing a brandy and some words of comfort. They found they agreed on a number of subjects – most notably their enormous dislike of sports.

Finally, in April, Betty and Don returned home, taking in Chicago and Denver on the way. (There was to be another promotional tour in 1948.) On her return Betty had to knuckle down to writing pieces she had promised to the *New Yorker* and *Atlantic Monthly;* she was also collaborating on a cookbook with Mary and working on her account of her time at Firland. Writing had become her new occupation.

Hollywood

The following month a whole new adventure beckoned: Hollywood. After a bidding war Universal-International Pictures had bought the film rights to the book for $100,000, with Betty receiving $10,000 for each remake or spin-off. The press ran a story that an ex-FBI agent sent by Chester Erskine, the director, had tracked Bob Heskett down to a Skid Row joint in San Francisco and offered him $1000 not to bring a lawsuit for being identified in the movie. The story had a basis in fact. Bob was indeed tracked down by an ex-FBI man but was found in Oakland, California. He was aware of Betty's success with *Egg*. He was told that if he agreed not to sue, he would be released from a $5,500 judgment against him that the court had awarded to Betty in 1944. Presumably, he signed, although in the event the surname Heskett never featured.

Betty warned Erskine not to 'arouse Peninsula people' by taking a planned trip to the Olympic Peninsula to scout for filming locations. She had been asked to accompany the crew but adamantly refused, declaring the attendant publicity a very bad idea and likely to stir up trouble. She had never set foot on the Peninsula since leaving and did not intend to, she said.

The press also reported that Betty had been invited to write the screenplay and to act in an advisory capacity under a contract for twelve weeks at $2,500 a week, although this appears to have been mere conjecture. However, in June she and Don and the girls set off for Hollywood for publicity purposes, picking up Mary and her husband from San Francisco on the way. Asked by the film company about her preferences in regard to interviews and stunts and so on, Betty replied that she had no objection to radio or interviews but shuddered at the word 'stunts'. She suggested that they clear any publicity events with Brandt & Brandt, 'as I inhale and exhale according to their directions.'

They arrived in Hollywood at dawn on 4 July, after being held up on the highway in a traffic jam of fishermen who had been out taking advantage of a low tide. According to the famous Hollywood gossip columnist Hedda Hopper, the film studio 'tossed an elaborate affair' for Betty at the Beverly Hills Club, attended by hundreds of people including movie stars Joan Bennett, Claudette Colbert, Mickey Rooney, Rosalind Russell and Danny Kaye – but the star of the party, according to Hedda, was Betty, with all the 'charm and naturalness' she had expressed in her book.

Betty with film star Claudette Colbert

Newspapers described Betty as an unbelievably pretty mother of two and reported that Anne, now eighteen and 'red-haired and vivacious', was being tested for a part in the film. She either didn't make it through the audition or the media were again playing a little free with their copy. To play Betty, the gossip columns were talking about Claudette Colbert or Joan Fontaine or even Shirley Temple, who was now grown up enough to be convincing as Betty at the age she had married Bob in *Egg*. Betty told the press she would rather have an older actress to play the part because she had written the book 'from a sophisticated slant'. In the end Betty herself did not write the script: she is not listed as one of the screenwriters. However, she did make enough of an impression at the studio to be invited back to appear personally in a 1947 trailer for the movie.

Coming down to earth with a bump on her return to Vashon, Betty commented that she was lucky she had her strength about her on seeing some of the Hollywood press items and realizing that the old French prostitute in one photograph was none other than herself.

§

As the book's sales continued to mount, Lippincott decided to invest in more advertising. The company took out a full-page spread in the 21 July 1946 issue of the *New York Times Book Review* to illustrate the book's astonishing progress. The by-then familiar cover showing Betty's smiling face was circled by cartoon sketches depicting scenes of *Egg*-crazed readers unable to put their copies down. A dancing couple read the book over one another's shoulders; a symphony conductor clutches his baton while his eyes stray down to *Egg* on the music stand; a bride at the altar, engrossed in the book, ignores minister and groom; curvy female beauty contestants parade past male judges who ignore their charms in order to laugh over *The Egg And I.* A banner across the ad reads 'Everything Else Is A Substitute' (referring no doubt to the use of egg substitute during the war).

That year *Egg* was to be the No. 1 seller for the whole of 1946 and the September Book-of-the-Month Club selection. It had sold a million copies in less than a year and over the following two years would be reprinted on an almost monthly basis. A gold leather-bound one millionth copy of the book, bearing a picture of a Buff Orpington setting hen, was eventually presented to Betty by the Governor of Washington State on behalf of publisher Lippincott (Betty's response: 'Thanks a million') and the Governor received a commemorative copy also. In the newsreel commemorating the occasion, entitled *Egg Brings Home Bacon*, Betty is slender and attractive in her dark tailored dress with leopard fur accents and matching hat. She gracefully signs the Governor's own copy of *Egg*, autographs actual eggs and gamely pins on an egg-and-chicken-feather corsage.

Courtesy Seattle's Museum of History and Industry

Bertram Lippincott himself, understandably taking a personal interest in a product that had sold to over a million customers, flew out from his Philadelphia publishing office to attend the occasion. He told the *Seattle Times* that although *Egg* was not the first book to reach the million mark, it was certainly the first to have reached it in less than a year, and the first to have taken so firm a grip on the national imagination.

That November *Reader's Digest* published an abridged version of *Egg* and sales went on climbing. Despite the continuing furor surrounding the family, Thanksgiving was celebrated in the usual Bard fashion: Mary and Betty sharing the cooking, one baking a ham and the other cooking the turkey, and one hosting the entire family of Bards for an additional meal later in the evening. With Betty's new-found fame things could not remain entirely normal, even so. Some time during the holiday period Betty left for Los Angeles to open an Anti-Tuberculosis Seal sale; she had not forgotten her old troubles, or those who continued to suffer. She was still using her fame to aid in the fight against tuberculosis over two years later: a 1948 newspaper photo shows her applying Christmas seals to gifts to promote a drive by the Tuberculosis Association. The dread disease could strike anyone, Betty warned, as she well knew from experience.

1947 rolled around with *The Egg and I* still hugely popular, and Betty no less so. January saw Betty and Don heading off to Hollywood again to make the planned trailer for the movie of *Egg*, which was now nearing completion at Universal-International Studios. Newspaper coverage of her trip made much of the fact that she had just made it onto the Associated Press list of its Women of the Year for 1946, along with luminaries such as the actresses Ingrid Bergman and Helen Hayes. Betty seemed more sophisticated on this visit, at least according to reporters, to whom she was a godsend with her witty one-liners. In the trailer ('HERE IT IS...the book that shook the world...with *Laughter!*') Betty looks very glamorous and her voice is low and mellifluous as she tells us how 'perfectly wonderful' and 'very, very funny' the movie is, and how one of the characters is that 'nasty, uncooperative stinker – Stove.' But she seemed uneasy under the heavy make-up and the *Seattle Times* noted that she appeared 'taut and nervous' while a technician checked the light meter. After the shoot she returned with some relief to her slightly less glamorous housewife/writer existence on Vashon, joking to her Brandt & Brandt agent Bernice that Hollywood was so tricky she and Don checked their napkins before use, for fear the napkin was really a contract to write for *Photoplay* and the gravy from her mouth would constitute a signature.

Betty then had to work hard on finishing her second book. This was to be the first of four in her children's series *Mrs Piggle-Wiggle*. Betty loved children and even when her own two were older she usually chose to surround herself with nieces and nephews, often to the detriment of her writing deadlines. She adored her sister Alison's sons Darsie and Bard, the first boys born to the Bard sisters, and they loved her in return. Alison wrote that Betty had once even saved the life of Alison's baby daughter by some timely advice. This love of small children was behind the decision to make her second publication one for the very young. J. B. Lippincott initially rejected the series, as had other publishers, but quickly reversed their decision after the phenomenal success of *Egg*.

Mrs Piggle-Wiggle came out in March. The book was based on some of the stories Betty used to tell Anne and Joan when they were little and then again to her nephews and nieces. She commented that she hoped the book sold, otherwise it would prove that all these years she had been boring children instead of amusing them. It did sell, and became a perennial children's classic. Mrs. Piggle-Wiggle is small and brown, with long brown hair and a magic hump on her back. She lives in an upside-down house, smells like cookies, and used to be married to a pirate who died after burying all his treasure in the back yard. She uses magic and a touch of psychology to cure the problems parents have with children, such as refusing to go to bed, not brushing teeth, picky eating, and never finishing tasks. Some of the children in the book have family names such as Anne and Joan and Mary, and a pair of brothers are Darsie and Bard just like Betty's nephews.

The *Mrs Piggle-Wiggle* series was illustrated by a variety of artists over the years, including Maurice Sendak of *Where the Wild Things Are* fame, and the books remained extremely popular with children for many decades. In the 1990s there was a TV series with Jean Stapleton, and Mrs Piggle-Wiggle herself has been transmuted into several international identities: *Fru Pille-Ville* in Denmark, *Mevrouw Piggle-Wiggle* in Holland, *Madame Bigote-Gigote* in France, *Fräulein Pudel-Dudel* in Germany, *Pigguru Uigguru Obasan* in Japan, *Tant Mittiprick* in Sweden, *Tetka Vsevedka* in Slovakia, and *Paní Láryfáry* in the Czech Republic.

Mary, Alison and Dede's children were, naturally, 'perfect angels and couldn't possibly have been the inspiration for any of these stories,' said Betty. Always a willing babysitter, Betty had written the book while the Vashon house crawled with children. 'I had so much help (from children) that I almost never got it finished,' she told an interviewer:

Most of my best writing has been done to the accompaniment of heavy breathing, sniffling and fat hands reaching up and poking the wrong key of the typewriter...

§

Continuing an eventful year, *The Egg and I* movie finally came out in May. Publicity prior to its release made the most of the egg theme. A press agent traveled the country carrying a Rhode Island Red hen, beak lipsticked and claws painted crimson, to represent Betty. Another gimmick called for hens and straw to be placed in theater lobbies for moviegoers to choose numbered eggs in hopes of a prize. Universal-International offered theaters a short cartoon trailer in which Henrietta Hen, pictured knitting in a hospital bed, hatches an egg that contains the instantly recognizable *Egg and I* book. Lippincott produced a special jacket for the book featuring the stars of the movie – and Stove – on the back cover. A board game in a green box similar to the book cover was 'as egg-citing as the book and the movie!' Betty and the stars of the film, meanwhile, became adept at autographing eggs. All the publicity, inevitably, was labeled 'eggsploitation'.

The movie exchanged the 1920s for the present day, with Bob a GI returned from combat in World War II. Betty was played by Claudette Colbert and Bob by Fred MacMurray, although Bob was called 'Bob MacDonald' in the film to gloss over the fact of Betty's divorce. Colbert and MacMurray had been paired in a number of movies previously but this was to prove their most popular by far. The studio also introduced a fictitious rival for Bob's affections, and appears to have labored under the misapprehension that chicken farmers' wives spend their working day larded in heavy make-up. Colbert's outfits, even her checkered country dresses, were by the sophisticated designer Adrian – a far cry from the simple items Betty had ordered from her Sears catalogs.

Ma Kettle was played by Marjorie Main, an actress who was reportedly obsessed with cleanliness and who objected to her role as a slatternly mother of thirteen feral children, but at least she received an Academy Award Nomination for Best Actress in a Supporting Role. (Her wardrobe was listed in the film's budget as 'Dirty House Dress'.) The movie cleaned the Kettles up considerably – in the book they are vulgar, stupid, dirty and foul-mouthed, even if rather affectionately depicted. 'Tits' Kettle did not appear.

Although Ma and Pa Kettle were only on screen for twenty-one minutes, Marjorie Main's gravelly voice and Percy Kilbride as a monosyllabic Pa made an enduring impression on audiences. They were such popular characters that eight more movies were made about them, churned out at Universal between 1949-1957 and taking on average three weeks to make for $400,000 or less. There are reports that the success of these spin-offs, which returned $35 million, saved Universal from bankruptcy. The relatively low-budget *Egg and I* had already put $5.5 million into Universal's bank account, a profit of $5.1 million. The critics panned the Kettle films but audiences laughed; Associate Producer Leonard Goldstein remarked sarcastically that nobody liked his pictures except the public. As for Betty, she loved the Ma and Pa Kettle series because for each movie she was of course sent a huge check, much enjoyed by all the family, for $10,000 per film.

The movie was a hit, despite some lukewarm reviews. The *New York Times* review by Bosley Crowther, for one, did not believe it did justice to Betty's writing:

For the nearest this watered-down rewrite gets to the solid soil is the dirt on the farm sets constructed on a studio soundstage. And the nearest it comes to realizing any of the diary's observation and wit is in a few farcified re-creations of some of its milder episodes.

In Crowther's opinion, this was possibly because the film's authors had been too wary of the censorship imposed by Hollywood's Motion Picture Production Code to attempt a real reflection of the franker passages in the book – or perhaps because they were simply intent on making a cozy, romantic version for female audiences. A good opportunity had been lost, he felt, to produce a delightful satire upon the back-to-the-farm movement – or, at least, a witty dissertation upon the life bucolic. Instead,

...most of the humor is artlessly derived from sure-fire situations which can be played for conventional farce. These are such things as Claudette Colbert, as a city wife moved to a farm, having her endless troubles with an incredibly perverse trick stove or falling down in the pig pen or dropping into the rain barrel off the barn roof. And most of the complicating interest is provoked in Miss Colbert's concern not for the welfare of the chickens but for the assurance of her breezy husband's love.

Claudette Colbert and Fred MacMurray also starred in a radio version of the film and *The Egg and I* ran as a CBS TV serial in 1951-52. The book likewise spawned not only the *Green Acres* TV show starring Eddie Albert and Eva Gabor but also a high school play and a musical, including one version staged by an all-African American cast.

§

It had become increasingly clear that Betty's new commitments required a base in Seattle; commuting from Vashon was too strenuous and time-consuming. In about June 1947 Betty and Don bought 905 E. Howe St., an old, solidly built Colonial home in the North Broadway area of Seattle's Capitol Hill. The house was located on a steep hillside with an expansive view of Lake Union and the Olympic Mountains, and was accessed by a long flight of concrete steps.

With all the money now at their disposal, and with the help of an architect, Betty and Don reshaped the old house and at the same time started some remodeling on their Vashon property. At Howe St. the original intention had been just to paint and paper and move in, but inevitably the work became more extensive. With two teenaged girls they decided they really needed three bathrooms instead of two, which meant a complete overhaul of plumbing and wiring. Having gone that far, Betty decided, they might as well knock out a wall or two and put in steel windows. They turned a sleeping porch with 'the most beautiful view in the world' into a study, furnishing it with a moss green couch, matching curtains and Chinese blinds. Betty did her writing on a business-like golden oak desk with an ordinary typewriter chair, despite people telling her she ought to have a fancy desk in chartreuse leather. She was now concentrating on finishing her Firland book, *The Plague and I,* and was trying to meet a deadline of 1 February the following year.

Courtesy Puget Sound Regional Archives

Despite work on the new book and all the remodeling, Betty's old sociable life continued. In August she had a visit from her uncle, Sydney's younger brother Jim Sanderson and his wife (he for whom Sydney had painted funny animals during a childhood illness). Nor did she neglect her bountiful garden back on Vashon, although Sydney had more or less taken over there. She planned to can the 'thousands of crates' of cherries picked from their Vashon orchards and left in cold storage. Then would come the harvesting of their Pacific Golds, a new Vashon Island variety of peach. These she planned to freeze or can using the open-kettle method. Betty also planned to scour the markets for little cucumbers for her family's famous dill pickles – '...the best pickles in the world,' she told an interviewer, giving the recipe for brine and vinegar over pieces of garlic and dill. Despite Betty's vitriolic comments about canning in *The Egg and I*, she certainly did plenty of it.

Betty and Don near their Capitol Hill home,
August 1947
Courtesy Seattle's Museum of History and Industry

Life for Betty at this point had settled into a rhythm of writing and domesticity, but with procrastination a recurring problem. She kept daily reminder books which often included an exhortation to herself: 'Write'. Existence was enlivened now and then by the continuing demands of her fame, and September saw one of her more famous advertising stunts. Eggs were often included in snapshots of Betty and the family and her new egg-related fame brought offers for product endorsement with a plug for her book usually thrown in. This time, in a promotion for the US Rubber Company, Betty was firmly clasped by Don as she leaned over to drop supposedly raw eggs from the 12th-story balcony of Seattle's Northwest Mutual Fire Insurance Building onto the rubber company's absorbent mats. Two catchers from the Seattle Rainiers baseball team stood by to catch the eggs after they miraculously rebounded unbroken. (The crowd of bystanders was then invited into the nearby Bon Marché to watch demonstrations of an exciting new product – television.) Advertising in later years included a spread for a Crosley refrigerator with Betty's picture appearing under the headline, 'The Egg and I Are Ten Times Happier!' Betty also advertised egg shampoo, candy eggs and Parker pens – yet more money rolling in.

However, Betty's financial situation was not as rosy as she thought it was. She had failed to realize the tax implications of her astonishing income. The royalty checks had not withheld for tax, and after an initial year of happy spending the income tax bill for 1946 probably came as a rude shock. To pay the bill Betty and Don took out a mortgage on the Howe St. house and then rented it out, and for a period Betty and Don even had to live in its basement apartment. Lippincott provided an advance to help meet the bill and Betty also received some assistance from both her attorney and her agent Bernice Baumgarten in managing her income, but it was a matter of some concern to Betty and Bernice that news of her financial woes might leak. The royalties continued to flow in, but Betty began to experience some of her old money worries and thereafter was never entirely free of them.

In Mary's opinion Don was to blame. She knew that her sister was good enough at math to be able to spot the errors in a bookkeeping record, but that in her financial affairs she nevertheless tended to defer to Don. Mary was not surprised that Don's decisions resulted in debt. A family friend remembered that after the job at Boeing came to an end Don no longer did any paid work, and that his many schemes often went wrong. Betty was occasionally impatient with him. After one quarrel with

Don she was the one who apologized but she told Mary that she had called him a 'spoiled, disagreeable, disorganized, money spending but not earning, disloyal bastard' – admitting that she hadn't really meant these things, but that she hoped he would recall a few of them. She once told Anne and Joan that she wanted to take swimming and driving lessons so that the next time she got mad at Don she could swim or drive away.

Some of Betty's frustrations with Don and her life in general found their way into an article that was never published. In her large family, she wrote, being an author, or 'authing', as they called it, rated as a hobby akin to pressing wildflowers:

> *First comes wifing, viz. cooking, cleaning, washing, ironing, smiling when angry, and using a pretty voice when I want to shriek. Then comes mothering or complete sublimation of my hurts and slights and insomnia and highstrungness and delicate condition due to my former bout with t. b.*

§

The Egg and I was to sell more than three million copies in hardback alone, with editions in thirty-two languages, and has never been out of print. The title coined a phrase that still remains lodged in the national consciousness of the English-speaking world. A seemingly endless string of books tried to cash in on the success of *Egg* with titles like *The Dredge and I* (a dull book about Alaska), *The Fish and I, The Cook and I, The Quilt and I,* and so on. Betty's comment was that she would rather be copied than be the copier.

Life for the whole family had now changed utterly, especially for Anne and Joan. These first few years of money and fame had been wonderful for them. On their visits to Hollywood the family had been given a private suite at the Beverly Hills Hotel and their own driver. Anne and Joan, used to country life on Vashon and not having much money, were thrilled with the suite and being able to order anything they liked, and doubly thrilled when they met the stars of the movie and the likes of Mickey Rooney, Elizabeth Taylor, and Clark Gable. In New York the four had stayed at the Algonquin Hotel and had gone to the Stork Club for Betty to be interviewed by the legendary newsman Walter Winchell. This lasted three or four hours until the girls finally fell asleep at three-thirty in the morning. They had been taken to Broadway shows, famous restaurants and sophisticated nightclubs like '21', and been introduced to many famous people. Sometimes they had worn their mother's brand new designer clothes pinned and rolled up while they joined in the autograph signings and radio interviews. As far as Anne and Joan were concerned the early period of Betty's fame was one long thrill.

The lugubrious Don appears to have been very unenthused by Betty's celebrity. He had turned into Mr. Betty MacDonald, and was forced to endure the perennial confusion between himself and Bob Heskett. In 1948 a journalist from the *New York Times* meeting Betty and Don for an interview described a silent Don gazing stolidly at his wife's veiled hat throughout (Betty, meanwhile, was 'nattier than the average ex-egg farmer' in a chic dress with rows of buttons and curvy black lapels). Don was never too sure about the road they eventually did build to the house, feeling his privacy would be threatened. Betty accused him of being a 'Big Black Future', but Don was proved right when a family of trippers one day appeared outside their kitchen window and asked Betty to pose for them taking a bite of egg.

As for Betty, her daughters as adults maintained that success did not alter her. She was characteristically modest about her achievements. In a letter to a fan Betty once remarked that writers were few and far between and it was therefore comparatively easy to get things published, and that her family frequently pointed this out to her. She told an interviewer:

There are some other things that had to do with the book selling a million copies. In the first place, Lippincott brought it out at a wonderful time – everyone was depressed by the war and they wanted to read something light, and that was very lucky for me. Also, the war ended just before the book came out, which was very fortunate, and then right afterwards they took the restrictions off the paper, which helped a great deal. (It's not) that I think that I'm such a wonderful writer that my next book will also sell a million copies because I know that there were too many things that had to do with God sitting on my shoulder that made this book a great seller.

She stayed the same Betty, despite the change in circumstances: she still wore sweatshirts and jeans and fed the chickens and did the ironing, and continued to love having company and doing things for her family. There were limits, however: Joan remembered once coming home and asking her mother to bake several dozen cookies for a school event – Betty's response was to ask Joan whether she wanted her to stay home and bake apple pies and smell like BO, or make a million dollars. But even with the royalties rolling in she kept her own and the family's feet on the ground: she insisted on the girls doing baby sitting as usual and taking summer and after-school jobs to earn their own money.

She was outstandingly generous with her new wealth. Betty was never one to spend money on herself but she loved giving presents, and she now gave each member of the family an exquisite gift and took several of them on paid trips to New York, Hollywood and Chicago. She was amused by her unexpected new affluence and the way the money kept pouring in. When her sister Alison's two-year-old son Bard drew a truck on the back of a slip of paper he had found, Betty howled with laughter – the slip of paper was a check for $8000. Betty gave him a hug: 'Bardo, now we know you're one of us.'

The generosity extended well beyond her immediate family. Betty's cleaning lady Mrs Hanson and her husband were given a free trip to Norway to see Mrs Hanson's parents, who had spent the war hidden in the mountains. Mrs Hanson was overwhelmed with gratitude, the more so because her parents died shortly after the visit. In Holland, when *The Egg and I* was translated into Dutch and 10,000 copies printed, Betty donated her royalties. Transferring money out of the country was not allowed because of all the rebuilding necessary after Holland's extensive war damage, and Betty requested that the royalties be used to help take care of Holland's cemeteries for American soldiers. A Betty MacDonald Foundation was established and in Opijnen, a quiet farming village where eight American airmen had lost their lives, the fund not only helped toward the upkeep of the American graves but also financed excursions and equipment for the village schoolchildren. The Foundation likewise contributed to a memorial plaque honoring the fallen American airmen and is mentioned on the plaque.

Betty also used her new-found fame to help her fellow islanders. In 1948 the local ferry line owner Alexander Peabody wanted to raise his rates and docked all the boats in Puget Sound for twenty-two days when local regulators refused to approve the increases. More than 115,000 commuters were unable to get to work. Making use of her celebrity, Betty tore into Peabody in a radio broadcast entitled *The Bad Egg and I*. Later in the year she and Don were photographed at a lively meeting of Vashon Islanders seeking to buy a couple of ferries to improve the service between Vashon and the southwest corner of Seattle. Betty's brother Cleve, by then a member of the Vashon Island Chamber of Commerce, was one of the speakers at the meeting.

§

Being famous was nevertheless to take its toll.

Throughout all the drama and publicity, the genuinely shy and modest Betty could not understand why anyone would want to meet her, let alone hear her make a speech. She would always say that she was nervous and unfunny and sounded just like Donald Duck. She was not comfortable being a celebrity.

If there's one thing I'd like, it would be to go back to the life before all this happened. It's all been fine and a wonderful experience, but the only good thing I can say about fame is that you can cash a check anywhere – the rest of it people can have.

Betty had achieved immense success – but at a price. The Mayor of Seattle may well have announced that he was 'reveling in the reflected glory and light of our great

Betty MacDonald' but Betty as the focus of this attention was not happy. In an article she described the jealousy and criticism provoked by her achievement. She could understand that her 'outrageous' success had been very galling to some writers who believed their own books were far better than hers, and couldn't see why theirs sold only a few thousand copies instead of Betty's million. She herself had never expected anything like it. The most she had hoped for was to get the 'damned thing' finished and published so that she wouldn't have to move off the island after telling everyone on the ferry that she was writing a book. A friend had warned her that if she made a great deal of money and spent it freely she would be called a show off, a 'try-to-be-grand'. If she made a great deal of money and saved it, she would be called stingy and a miser.

He said that I would encounter envy and jealousy where I least expect it and instead of getting my feelings hurt I should learn to brace my feet and let the blows glance off. I have tried and tried but...I still cannot understand why people will crawl for miles over broken glass just to tell me how hideous I look.

The effort to lead a normal life, entertain her guests on Vashon and yet be famous and keep writing was exhausting. In a letter she wrote tiredly,

...in spite of myself I seem to be running an establishment which is a cross between a rest home and Grand Central Station. All my family and friends are as brown as nuts and ruddy with health, while I am dead tired and as white as a grub because I have not been out of the kitchen since April. 'I'm a genius,' I keep screaming and my family says, 'Just get on with the cooking and let's not be temperamental'.

Betty received numerous invitations to speak at women's clubs and she told Blanche that women who up until then scarcely knew she existed suddenly become her best friends and would insist she come to give a talk. Other women were critical. Needing a pair of stockings one day, she asked Don to stop the car at a department store while she ran in. She wasn't very dressed up and in the short time it took to buy the stockings she heard a woman say to her friend, 'There's Betty MacDonald. Look at the awful clothes she has on.' Betty complained to Blanche that her privacy was out of the window.

Fame was not for Betty, but for the rest of her life she was never to escape it.

I think fame is the most appalling thing that can happen to you. I certainly think the old saying is true – 'Get your head above the masses and you'll get stones thrown at you.' You have to be thick-skinned to take it.

As for the money, she professed herself indifferent. Writing about her attitude to money for *Cosmopolitan* in June 1949 she declared that if she had to choose between being rich or poor, she would choose poor, pointing out that she spoke from experience. At times in her life she had had plenty of money and at other times none; the times with none were by far the happiest. She wrote that she always spoke with such nostalgia about the Depression that Anne and Joan would ask if there was likely to be another Depression in their own lifetime so that they, too, could have some fun. For Betty, having money could never compensate for lack of charm; rich people who were rude or dull or brutal were still rude or dull or brutal. She claimed to be just as happy in a flattering $1.89 Sears Roebuck housedress as she would be in $750 Schiaparelli. In fact expensive clothes made her nervous because they made her feel guilty when the money could have been put to better use, such as for a down payment on a home. She professed not to feel the need for security that most Americans seemed to want at that time, and believed that financially secure people were the most miserable, forever worrying about what they were spending when they might be saving. In the past few years she and the family had cheerfully spent, eaten, drunk, and traveled away the interest on about ten million dollars, and thoroughly enjoyed doing it, she said. If you did have money, it was for spending and enjoying yourself, not saving. None of her family had ever had any sense with money and nobody had more fun.

§

Despite these declarations, of course, Betty's new income had been received with open arms. In the first heady period of her success Betty wrote to an old friend from Firland that she was suddenly welcome in all the big stores:

Bests who wouldn't even let me pay cash in their store last Christmas are imploring me to open an account and Frederick & Nelson instead of holding a conference of the entire store every time I charge a handkerchief, o.k. <u>anything</u>. I don't give a damn for the fame – it is the freedom from flinching when the phone rings – the ability to stare rudely at credit managers which thrills me.

With the initial flow of money Betty paid off all the mortgages on the shingled house in 15th Avenue that the family had somehow clung to throughout the Depression. Sydney then sold it, deriving a modest income from the sale. Betty and Don also settled their own mortgage on the

Vashon house (although remortgaging a few years later) and improved the house as they had once dreamed. With the proceeds from book and film they purchased the blast furnace, a farm of ten acres adjoining their own land on the hill above, and the desperately wanted driveway to replace the one-and-a-half mile trail to the main road. Don bought a small bulldozer and carved the switchback road into the hillside himself. The property remained quite private, despite Don's misgivings. They put in a $180 septic tank under one terrace but eventually rebuilt the terraces anyway, replacing the existing cedar with bluestone. The bathroom was modernized and a new bathroom for the girls installed for $800. A small suite was built for Sydney, the kitchen relocated, and a cottage constructed for guests. Betty got her fireplaces and the girls got radiant heat under the floors, plus the yearned-for charge account at the Vashon drug store, kept to under $25 a month – which at the time seemed more like $2500. Don was granted his case of very old, very expensive imported Scotch, his case of mushrooms and the big locks for his closet (which for some reason came without keys, an omission naturally discovered just too late).

On the ten-acre farm the family started to raise pigs, lambs, turkeys, geese, cows, chickens, and mallard ducks, eventually selling their own milk, eggs, peaches and cherries.

Later, in 1948, the MacDonalds built a huge, 1900s-style barn looking out to Puget Sound. In a chicken house adjoining the barn Betty went back to looking after thousands of chickens, this time with the more amenable Don. To prevent the chickens from attacking each other, there were stories that Don, rather creatively if true, fitted them all with eyeglasses designed to keep their attention focused on their food. He marketed the eggs on the island

and at Pike Place Market in Seattle, no doubt capitalizing just a little on Betty's egg fame.

Courtesy Puget Sound Regional Archives

Success changed her life in many ways, but perhaps most importantly *The Egg and I* turned Betty into a professional writer. She had lost her job in order to write it, and now her career path was obvious: she had to keep writing, and also to improve at it. Betty had a poor opinion of her own writing ability, which in her estimation consisted of taking some small incident and padding it out with lies and descriptions. There had been a lot of revision work necessary on *Egg*, for instance. 'I had to rewrite the entire book – I had written it in journal style,' she told the *Seattle Times* in 1950.

To start with, Betty wrote frantically against advances, trying to keep up with the bills. She knew she was a procrastinator and said that the hardest thing she had to do as a writer was force herself to sit at her typewriter and get to work. She always felt under pressure, forever fending off domestic disaster, housework, gardening, guests, children, relatives, grandchildren – all the things that gave her the life she loved to write about. Her old friend Blanche was with her one day when Betty was playing with children rather than working on her next book as she should have been. The telephone rang. It was Betty's agent, asking for the expected chapters. Betty came clean about what she was actually doing and she was asked if she wanted to be a one-book author spending the rest of her life over a sink and an ironing board, or whether she wanted to be known for other works as well. She got the message.

In later years, after she and Don had moved to a ranch in California, a male writer once told her that every day when he got up he immediately sat down and wrote for four hours. Betty's retort:

I get right out of bed and make coffee, squeeze oranges, fix breakfast, wash dishes, make beds, sort laundry, make a grocery list, decide what to have for dinner, answer the phone, feed cats, talk to feed salesmen, make more coffee for road crew, talk to cowboys, get lunch, do dishes, answer four letters from people who want me to speak, then write...it is now 4:30 and almost time to start dinner.

Her advice to writers: be born a man.

Her real advice to aspiring writers was to read, read, read, and Betty's daughters remembered their home always overflowing with books. When Betty disciplined the girls for some misdemeanor she made them sit on their big front deck on Vashon and read books that she thought would be good for them to get to know. She made sure they read as much as they could, and they had to produce reports on what was read. Betty considered Kipling one of the best authors for the very young and also liked Doctor Doolittle for small children. She numbered among her own favorites Dickens, the Brontës, Sinclair Lewis, Willa Cather, Truman Capote, Elizabeth

Enright, Angela Thirkell, Katherine Anne Porter and the early works of John Steinbeck. She liked Baudelaire, Huxley, and Dostoyevsky. A particular favorite was children's writer E. B. White, author of *Charlotte's Web* and *Stuart Little*, who also wrote for adults and whom Betty adored.

Despite the difficulty of getting down to it Betty did love being a writer, and took it seriously. She hated 'trite and shop-worn phrases' – they nauseated her, she once declared. She joined Seattle's oldest writing club, the Seattle Free Lances, and attended writers' conferences. At the Northwest Writers' Conference of September 1947 Betty asked the famous Southern writer Eudora Welty – who like Betty had once done work for Roosevelt's Works Progress Administration during the Depression – to autograph her copy of Eudora's *Delta Wedding*. Eudora obliged with 'From the *Delta* to the *Egg'*.

Betty never had a special place to work and often bemoaned the fact. Even after becoming a famous author she didn't have even a tiny corner to call her own in the house on Vashon. At different times she wrote in the basement, at the kitchen table, at the dining room table, or on a tiny rackety typewriter table in her bedroom. After moving to California she wrote in the teeming bunk house of their ranch. All I ask, she told her family, is one quiet spot where I can write:

This is a lie, of course, and they know it. What I really want is a million dollars so I won't ever have to write another word.

Betty answered and dealt kindly with even the most bizarre fan letters, which were often long, dull, boring missives giving or pleading for advice on all kinds of subjects. Some fans were fairly rude, telling Betty they hadn't realized she was 'so huge' (Betty was 5' 6 ¾") or 'soooo fat'. Some fans requested financial aid, or collaboration or help in getting their funnier and better books published; some wanted to visit or to find out how to cook chicken, ride horses, care for cows, or raise children. One woman reportedly wanted advice on writing about her trip to Holland, to be called *The Hague and I*. Asked for general writing advice Betty encouraged the creation of an outline before starting, and singled out reading as the best help for new writers. She also joked that what she ought to be advising was a big mortgage and plenty of coffee.

Many letters, from both adults and children, were simply to thank her for the enormous pleasure her books gave. Each letter received a response, in person to start with but eventually through an assistant. In one of her earliest replies to a fan Betty described her own doings and her family at length and invited the fan to visit, even giving out her phone number. In time she became a little less open-armed but she always distinguished between the sometimes very proper, stiff fan letters she received and the kind written on cheap paper, perhaps a little smudged, but with warm and sincere expressions of love for her books. These she cherished.

When with the passage of time Betty was unable to answer every letter personally she took on secretaries to help with the job, creating appropriately named templates for the responses. A delayed reply to someone used the *Dear Fandelay* answer, which explained that 'life here is very hectic'. Enthusiastic fans received the *Dear Mrs. Fanilike*: 'One of the nicest things about my success has been the letters I have received from people like you who have been kind enough to take the time to tell me that you enjoyed my writing.' There was a template for a polite refusal to suggested engagements, which Betty was usually too busy to accept, and a template for answering hopeful writers looking for advice. Responses to children for their 'darling letter' were signed with 'Love.'

She was inevitably sent unsolicited manuscripts but Brandt & Brandt discouraged her from collaborating, or even reading them, lest she write something similar later and be accused of plagiarism.

§

Betty's next adult book to be published came out in 1948: *The Plague and I,* the story of her time at Firland. After the success of *Egg* her agents and publishers had begun pressing her for a sequel at around the time that *Mrs. Piggle-Wiggle* was launched, and Betty was conscious that she needed more money. She decided to resurrect her old manuscript about the sanatorium. She had been bitter when she entered, she wrote to another former patient, unhappy much of the time and longing to get out, but she would not have missed such a remarkable experience for the world. It was a book she had to write, and it turned out to be her own favorite.

Betty also seems to have felt a strong urge to educate others regarding the disease. Talking about *Plague* before its appearance she warned that too few people recognized the symptoms of tuberculosis early enough. When they did, she continued, they needed a hammer to the head to get them to do anything about it. In *Plague* she endeavored to include up-to-date information and yet keep it bright enough so that people would read it; her editors congratulated her, commenting that in anyone else's hands it would have been a very dull subject.

But the book had been an uphill climb for Betty, despite having engaged a former room-mate at Firland, Gwen Smith Croxford, to type out the manuscript. Lippincott's had been obliged to telegraph her about meeting her deadline, which she appears to have missed, and then started sending people out to see her. With the editors hanging around she forced herself to finish it. (Though even more pressing than editors, she told a meeting of the Seattle Free Lances writing club at the time, was a $93,000 income tax payment hanging over her head.)

The book was published with a photo on the back cover of a vibrant Betty pruning a rose bush. She had a point to make:

I wanted something out-doorsy and healthy looking to prove to my readers, or rather 'reader', that I had not dictated the book from an oxygen tent.

This time the book was condensed and serialized by *Good Housekeeping*, in their August, September and October 1948 issues. Betty told a friend that it had been sweetened and cleaned up beyond recognition to placate the magazine's advertisers. 'Son of a bitch' had become 'rather unpleasant' while 'Jesus Christ' had appeared as 'dear, dear'. The book, too, had been subject to some excision: two of the nurse characters, despite the demise of their originals, had had their sharp edges removed.

Plague is just as funny as *The Egg and I* although more somber, and interesting in its own right as a historic first-hand account of the rest cure in a TB sanatorium before the disease became curable by antibiotics. A *New York Times* review praised the artistry of her style and the 'infectious gaiety of her perspective' but also her sensitive understanding. The *Saturday Review* deemed Betty one of those rare human beings who could see the funny side of everything that happens to them, and one of those rare authors who could make her experiences equally funny on the page.

The medical community, on the other hand, were less impressed. One doctor refused to endorse the book, fearing that Betty's grim picture of hospital life and impersonal treatment might frighten off some patients from entering a sanatorium.

Plague made the *New York Times* weekly best-seller list and continued to sell well, although not to the extent of *The Egg and I;* Lippincott had put less into advertising, perhaps because the work failed to generate the advance excitement of the earlier work. Today the book is possibly the least known of Betty's works.

There was a less happy ending for Betty's assistant Gwen, who in 1953 was forced to return to Firland after twelve years of near-normal life. In 1956 she married a former patient and was granted a seventy-two-hour pass from the sanatorium for her honeymoon; sadly, she then returned to Firland, still in ill-health. Betty was the lucky one.

After the *Egg* movie came out Betty had made a visit to Firland, despite her reluctance about returning, to attend a screening for the ambulatory patients. She and Don dined with some of her former doctors and Betty gave a talk in the same auditorium where in *Plague* she watches Greta Garbo die of consumption in *Camille*. She promised the patients that her next book would be about Firland, and it was.

While Betty was at work on *The Plague and I* new antibiotics began to prove highly effective in treating tuberculosis. Deaths at Firland fell from 31% in 1948 to just 6 % in 1954.

The White Plague had been beaten.

§

The girls, meanwhile, were growing up. Although very bright, Anne had never liked school but she agreed to graduate and then make up her own mind about college. After graduation she got a job in the advertising department of a large store, living in Seattle and sharing an apartment with another girl. On 22 January 1949, at the age of twenty, she married Donald John Strunk in Seattle's Blessed Sacrament Church. The bride was resplendent in an ivory silk brocade dress and an illusion veil fixed to a brocaded headdress with stephanotis flowers. Don gave Anne away and Joan was one of the bridesmaids, who all wore Anne's favorite color blue. Even the wedding cake at the breakfast hosted by Mary had blue frosting, and blue was the color of the car the young couple received from Betty and Don as a wedding present. Almost immediately Anne set about having children and Betty at the age of forty-two became a very young grandmother. Naturally she loved having a grandchild and the little family were frequent visitors on Vashon.

Later that spring Betty and Don leased out the Seattle house they had poured so much money into and retreated back to Vashon. In addition to their financial worries Betty had been finding it more and more difficult to meet her writing deadlines among all the distractions of the city. She was trying to finish another *Mrs Piggle-Wiggle* book for Lippincott in March and also had an article due for a national monthly magazine. By April 1949 they were back on the island and Betty started writing from 6 am to 6 pm, a rigorous schedule she had never been able to keep to in Seattle. The joint cookbook with Mary was due out in May, but for whatever reason the project appears to have fizzled out and the cookbook never appeared. Despite the twelve-hour writing schedule there was still a stream of visitors and Betty joked about running a small hotel. By July, though, she had completed the second *Mrs Piggle-Wiggle*, plus four articles for national magazines, and was making good progress on her third book for adults, *Anybody Can Do Anything*.

As ever, she interspersed the writing with enthusiastic gardening and animal raising. She told the audience at a luncheon given in her honor at Frederick & Nelson's department store in October that she and Don now had 5000 chickens, three cows, twelve pigs, two lambs, and some ducks and turkeys. Don had built a house for their two helpers back of their own. Their hibiscus, gardenias and bougainvillea, sent up from California, were flourishing despite the climate and Betty was looking forward to having an avocado patch. (By now Betty was an acknowledged gardener as well as writer: the previous year she had been asked to open the Rose Society Show at the Olympic Hotel in Seattle.)

The writing was also going well and Betty was extremely gratified when she learned that the new *Mrs Piggle-Wiggle* had been made a textbook at the University of Georgia's creative writing classes as an example of writing for juveniles. She had nearly finished *Anybody Can Do Anything* (anticipating reviews along the lines of 'No, anybody can't'). Her publishers had also asked her to write a novel, so she was trying some plotting when she wasn't writing. Before she started on it in earnest, she and Don went to visit a ranch after a request from a national magazine to write an article on dude ranching, but the visit may also have been part of early planning for their eventual move to California.

Meanwhile, the retreat to Vashon in early 1949 had an unexpected consequence. That summer Betty and Don leased out their Howe St. home to five young FBI agents whom they also invited out to Vashon for weekends. One of the agents was Girard (Jerry) Keil, and Joan on a visit home was smitten. After graduating from Seattle's Garfield High School Joan had attended the University of Washington, living in a sorority house but coming home frequently to Vashon to get some home cooking. Joan and Jerry married on 21 January 1950, with the wedding breakfast again at Mary's. The ceremony was held in candlelight and this time the theme was pink: blush-pink tapers, camellias, carnations and stocks, and pale pink orchids carried by beautiful Joan. Her gown was brocaded silk with a portrait neckline and tiny covered buttons to the waist; her illusion veil was attached to a cloche of the same brocaded silk with clusters of pearl orange blossoms on either side. Anne was matron of honor. Mother of the bride Betty was smart in a beige suit with beaver accessories and a brown and green orchard corsage. Just like Anne and Don, the young couple soon set about starting a family.

Joan and Jerry initially lived in Los Angeles, and Betty and Don would visit them there and introduce them to their old Hollywood contacts from the days of filming *The Egg and I*. One night the four visited the home of Ray Stark, Betty's agent in Hollywood, to meet the comedienne Fanny Brice. Ray was married to Fanny Brice's daughter and because Betty loved Fanny Brice so much she wanted Joan and Jerry to meet her. They had dinner, met yet more stars and then, in typical Hollywood style, watched a movie shown on a large pull-down screen.

On their visits to Joan, who missed them, Betty and Don discussed buying property on the West Coast. In the event, Joan and her husband returned to the Seattle area within the year, but a move to California remained on Betty's mind.

§

In 1950 Betty finally published *Anybody Can Do Anything,* her work about her family's troubles, and joys, during the years of the Depression. The initial plan had been to write the book jointly with Mary, but the idea was discouraged by Betty's agent Bernice Baumgarten, who felt that it would be easier for Betty to write about her sister than for Mary to write truthfully about herself. The book would also sell better under Betty's name. In the event Betty found it hard going to write about Mary because of their close relationship and the domineering role Mary played in her life. It was hard, too, to relive the harsh experiences of the Depression and at the same time be entertaining. The writing was a long struggle with much revision needed, and Betty was unsure if there was really a book in it. 'One chapter I think is amusing - ' she wrote to Bernice, ' - but the point is who gives a Goddamn where I worked and why?' Bernice helped keep her equilibrium. As Betty told a *Seattle Times* reporter,

She's absolutely honest and never spares me. I was afraid when she called about this latest book. I had sent her twelve chapters and she sent all but two back and said, 'This isn't you.' So I wrote them over.

The *Saturday Evening Post* serialized the book in four installments under the title *It All Happened to Me*, with the usual toning down that Betty by now had come to expect. When their editors wanted to introduce the word 'classy' to describe a department store, however, Betty retorted that she would rather be dead than ever use such a word. 'Hash-slinging' for Betty's original 'prostitution' was rejected with the same scorn.

The magazine's photographer came to Vashon Island and, just as in the early days of Betty's fame, he lived with the MacDonalds for a week while following Betty and the family around. However, this time Lippincott did little in the way of publicity, and Betty herself had tired of book tours. There was no traveling around the country, no signing of copies, even locally in Seattle bookstores. The book had been hard work, and Betty was exhausted and worried about finances.

Anybody is a truly funny description of the various jobs Betty was pushed into by Mary and the Bards' stratagems for staying afloat during the Depression, but it pulls no punches about the realities of being poor during the 1930s. As always in Betty's books, though, there is a thread of hope and optimism that relieves the touches of gloom and Betty's writing is as witty and evocative as ever. *Anybody* was eventually adapted as a Broadway play, in the contract for which Anne and Joan were promised first-row center seats for each performance, but the play was never produced.

Betty had been conscious, after the success of her earlier books, that the book's reception had 'an awful precedent' hanging over it. But Bert Lippincott thought it better than either *Egg* or *Plague* and called it 'one of the few great books of humorous Americana'. The way it captured the

American scene was reminiscent of Mark Twain and early Sinclair Lewis, he told Betty. The *New York Times*, for its part, was impressed by the way Betty had transmuted her grim experiences into 'rollicking reminiscence'. It made the *New York Times* weekly best-seller list but sales thereafter were slow.

Despite the disappointing return, *Anybody* was bid for by more than one Hollywood producer but nothing came of it. Columbia Pictures, for one, worried about libel, and in their negotiations with Bernice demanded that anyone appearing in the book sign a written release. While Bernice recognized that this might have been possible as regards family members, she saw that it was a condition that could not ultimately be met.

'My natural inclination when I finish writing a book is to pull a cover over my head and forget it,' Betty said in August. She carried on writing, trying to do as much as she could in the mornings. The stream of guests still continued – the MacDonalds consumed a case of coffee every two weeks and there had been comments about hoarding when people saw Don buying the case at the grocery store. The constant influx of guests made writing difficult.

My downfall is coming downstairs to breakfast. We have a great big kitchen with a fireplace, and it is always jammed with people. You work hard under conditions like that, but difficulties really are an asset to a writer. You can feel awfully sorry for yourself, but on the other hand I have to be fresh and stimulated, and people do that to me.

She was planning her next project, two new books for children. Her previous ones were still extremely successful; *Mrs Piggle-Wiggle* was now being used at the famous Menninger psychiatric clinic as part of its therapy for the young. She just about had time to produce something new – Anne was now expecting her second baby and Joan was expecting her first, but there was a little space before Betty was swamped by serious grandmother duty.

'My agent has my writing time all figured out,' she explained to an interviewer from the *Seattle Times*. 'With Anne having a baby in December and Joan in March, that gives me September, October and November to write this next one. It probably will be ready for spring of '51. It may be the *Nancy and Plum* stories I used to tell to Anne and Joan. I'd get so fascinated with them I couldn't stop and they went on and on.' At this point Betty still hadn't decided whether to write up *Nancy and Plum,* which in fact dated right back to her childhood when she used to tell the stories to Mary in bed at night. She also had something in rough manuscript form called *Cocoanut and Gingersnap,* about a fairy and a brownie, yet another of a series she used to tell Anne and Joan when they were little.

As well as her writing she was still kept busy answering the usual ten to twenty-five fan letters a day, often from children. *Plague* had brought her much correspondence from sanatoriums and even a letter from a doctor in Japan. But *Anybody* had brought the best fan letters yet.

People say it's an inspiration because I've been able to weather all kinds of storms. I've had only one crank letter on it so far – from the biggest I-hate-men-if-I'd-ever-had-any who said all men ever wanted out of women on jobs was work and more work. The Post editors asked if I wanted to answer it. I said that as far as I was concerned the typing was nice.

Betty was making a very successful life for herself as a writer, and was mostly happy doing so, despite continuing money worries and the exigencies of being famous. But a shadow was falling over Betty's achievements and her delight in her new grandchildren. As early as 1947 the Bishop family, the originals for the feckless Kettles in *The Egg and I,* had sued for libel. The case came to court in 1951 and once again Betty was in the spotlight.

Betty and the Law

Courtesy Seattle's Museum of History and Industry

BETTY tensely faced her interrogator, plaintiffs' attorney George H. Crandell. It was the afternoon of 15 February 1951 in King County Superior Court in Seattle.

Betty's defense against the charge of libel was to maintain that she had made up the whole of *The Egg and I* and that it had no basis in reality. Crandell's tack was of course to prove the exact opposite: that Betty *had* based her book on the people and places she knew around the area of Chimacum where she had lived with Bob Heskett.

He began by asking Betty if her book's description of the 'Kettle place' did not fit the Albert Bishop farm which adjoined the ranch where she had lived from 1927 to 1931.

'No,' Betty replied. 'I wrote the book and I wasn't writing about it.'

Pressed about other details regarding the Bishop farm, Betty responded: 'I haven't the faintest idea. I haven't been there for twenty years.'

Twenty minutes of stiff cross-examination followed, question after question, until suddenly Betty was overcome. Breaking down in tears, she ran from the stand. **Betty MacDonald Flees Courtroom While Under Cross-Examination** screamed the headlines in the local press.

The following morning Betty's torment resumed as Crandell drove on with his questioning.

She insisted that 'it would have to be a coincidence' if her descriptions in *Egg* of Paw Kettle, the Kettles' farm and the Kettle farmhouse parlor in any way resembled Albert Bishop, his farm and the Bishops' parlor.

'You've been in the Bishops' parlor?' Crandell asked.

'No, I never was,' Betty answered.

'Do you remember Mrs Bishop?'

'No, I do not. I just remember her as a nice woman.'

Betty did not have 'the faintest idea' as to when she first met Albert Bishop or 'the faintest recollection' of what he looked like. When Crandell asked Betty if, before she was married and while living with her mother near the Bishop farm, she had ever attended a dance with Albert Bishop's son Walter, Betty replied: 'One dance which my brother made me go to.' Asked by Crandell to elaborate, Betty explained that her brother had said that 'if I didn't go people would think I was snooty.' She stated that she had been a good friend of Janet Bishop, the wife of Albert's son Herbert, but denied ('at the risk of being unkind') that Janet was the model for the beautiful, dancing-eyed Jeanie Kettle in *Egg*.

She insisted to the court that she did not describe Port Ludlow as 'Docktown,' Chimacum as 'Crossroads' or Port Townsend as 'Town'. 'In all my descriptions of towns I tried to picture a typical town,' she maintained. She was writing about 'an imaginary place in an imaginary country'.

During this second day under cross-examination Betty remained calm as she parried Crandell's questions. There were no further breakdowns, and the ordeal finally drew to a close. The lawyers' summing up and the verdict of the jury were still to come.

§

Lippincott's lawyers had been right to fear the possibility of libel when *Egg* was still in manuscript. Betty in about 1945 had informed them that if basing a character on some characteristics of a real person constituted libel, then all of her characters were libelous. She had gaily told Lippincott that the real Mrs. Kettle – at that point called Mrs. Basket in her manuscript – was in reality the kindly if profane Mrs. Bishop; that Mr. Bishop had a lisp and used to borrow from his neighbors; and that Crowbar, Clamface and Geoduck were based on three actual Indian friends of Bob's. The brawling, indecent Indian picnic she described in *Egg* had indeed taken place in actuality but had been even more obscene. In fact either Lippincott or Betty's agent Bernice Baumgarten had suggested changing the name from Basket because it was too like Bishop. Betty suggested Kettle, and just before publication Lippincott followed the example of the *Atlantic Monthly* serialization and changed all the place names.

Betty at the time had been willing to make the changes, although she wanted to show the magnificence of the country 'in comparison [with] the unsavoriness of its inhabitants,' she wrote to Bernice in 1945. But, she had continued, perhaps her upbringing and youth and inexperience, and loneliness, had made her think people worse than they were: now that she was older, she might find them more amusing than horrifying. Maybe she should not attempt to depict reality at all:

Perhaps the book would have a better flavor if I were to forget the truth and make the people less like the ignorant, immoral, amoral, unmoral, foul mouthed group they were, and more folksy and quaint. If depicting the people as they were is libelous, then by all means let's show them as they weren't.

Despite Lippincott's precautions two lawsuits were eventually filed by residents from Chimacum. In both, the family of Albert and Susanna Bishop claimed that the Kettle and other characters in the book had been based on them and that they had been identified in their community as the real-life versions of those characters and therefore subjected to ridicule and humiliation.

The first lawsuit was filed in March 1947 by the Bishops' eldest son Edward and his wife Ilah, whose property had abutted Betty's mother's farm. Alleging that they were Betty's models for her characters Mr. and Mrs. Hicks, another set of neighbors in the book, the Bishops asked $100,000 in damages. The book was libelous and an invasion of their right to privacy, they claimed, and as a result of its publication they had been exposed to ridicule, hatred, and contempt.

On September 27, 1947, the case was ordered to trial after King County Superior Judge Hugh Todd issued a memorandum opinion denying Betty's motion to dismiss. The judge ruled that certain statements in the book, if true, were libelous. He pointed out that although truth is a defense in actions of this kind, the publication of such facts or conversation could be an invasion of the rights of privacy. If so, the plaintiffs were entitled to recover damages, regardless of truth or untruth.

At times the judge's lengthy statement read like a rather strange review of the book.

The story is intriguing, the style is original and fascinating, the diction in places perfect and in others not parloresque – (I think I made that word up) – the authoress tells you that here we, too, have the hillbillies of the wilds of Kentucky and of the mountains of Tennessee.

But the first case never went to court. After two years of legal maneuvering, and just as the suit was moving toward a jury trial, the two sets of attorneys jointly filed a stipulation for dismissal on 4 May 1949. On 28 May the case was dismissed, settled out of court for $1500.

The second and more extensive lawsuit was filed against Betty, Don, her publisher Lippincott, the Bon Marché (the Seattle department store which had promoted and distributed the book) and Pocket Books, which had issued a 25-cent paperback edition. Bon Marché was later dismissed as a defendant on the basis that another company operated the store, and Pocket Books was apparently never even served with legal papers and so did not appear. This time nine other members of the Bishop family were demanding $100,000 each in damages (although one son and his wife asked for the same sum jointly) while Raymond H. Johnson, who claimed he had been portrayed as Crowbar, the Native American character, demanded $75,000. By the time the jury began deliberating, however, the total amount of damages sought was reported as the lower figure of $500,000, as two causes of action had been ruled out. In any case the plaintiffs' lawyers had mistakenly entered the Pocket Books edition of the book as evidence rather than the bestseller hardcover versions, meaning that any damages awarded would have to be based on the lesser Pocket Books sales.

The case was heard at King County Superior Court in Seattle in early February 1951 before a jury and Judge William J. Wilkins, who had been one of the judges at the Nuremberg Trials. Betty's attorney George Guttormsen was an old friend of Mary's, an usher at her wedding in 1934, and a former football captain at the University of Washington. Betty had known him since she was fourteen and referred to him as an honest and smart lawyer. (Guttormsen had a link with another famous Seattle writer, Mary McCarthy, author of 'The Group', the 1963 best-seller about the lives of eight Vassar women. Mary McCarthy revealed in a memoir that she and George, whom she described as a good-looking intellectual, had had a brief affair in 1931 when George was just out of law school. Betty in her turn had a link with Mary McCarthy: both had attended the Cornish School.)

The plaintiffs were elderly Albert Bishop and his many offspring – sons Herbert, Wilbur, Eugene, Arthur, Charles, and Walter Bishop, and daughters Edith Bishop Stark and Madeline Bishop Holmes – and Raymond Johnson. The Bishop family alleged that they had been depicted by Betty MacDonald as the easy-going, slovenly Kettle family in *The Egg And I,* and Johnson alleged that he was depicted as Crowbar. As a result, they claimed, they had been subjected to ridicule because readers identified them with those characters.

Susanna Bishop, the alleged inspiration for Ma Kettle, was no longer living. She had died in 1937, heartbroken after the death of her youngest child Kenneth by drowning. Albert Bishop, who claimed he was the model for Pa Kettle, was aged eighty-seven and too ill to come to court, but the rest of the family attended each day of the trial. Betty and Don were also present, as were Joan and husband Jerry at least some of the time. The jury was made up of three women and nine men. Judge Wilkins had a copy of *The Egg and I* in court and followed passages as they were read aloud during questioning.

For the book to be found libelous, the jury would have to agree both that the Bishops were the Kettles and that Johnson was Crowbar, and that Betty's comic depictions of incidents involving Crowbar and the Kettles exceeded actuality. The crux therefore was whether incidents that happened to the Kettles in the book had also happened to the Bishops in real life, and during the opening stages of the trial questioning of the Bishop family focused on this point.

Taking questions from his own attorney, Wilbur Bishop stated that the home of the Albert Bishop family between Chimacum and Port Ludlow, Jefferson County, was about a mile from the place where Betty MacDonald had lived around twenty years before. The attorney read a passage from the book describing an incident in which Pa Kettle set out to burn some trash in the backyard and ended up burning down the barn. He asked his client if his father, Arthur Bishop, had done this. Bishop said he had. A number of other Jefferson County residents testified that the Kettles were clearly recognizable as the Bishops.

Annie McGuire, a very lively elderly widow, claimed that upon reading the book she not only immediately recognized the Kettles as the Bishops but thought that she herself was the character Mary MacGregor (described by Betty as having 'fiery red, dyed hair, a large dairy ranch and a taste for liquor').

Courtesy Seattle's Museum of History and Industry

Raymond Johnson testified that he recognized himself as the character called Crowbar, and that the characters Clamface and Geoduck were actual people who used those names. He said that he had never been known by any other name and that after the book came out people had teased him by calling him 'Double Yolk'. Johnson also claimed that he had gone hunting with Betty's husband Bob just as Betty had described in *The Egg And I*.

There was more than enough in these various testimonies to give the jurors pause. However, evidence also existed that the Bishops had acknowledged, and tried to profit from, their alleged depiction in *The Egg and I*. One witness described being approached by Walter Bishop to go into business with him to build a dance hall at Port Townsend and organize a tour of 'the Kettles' because there was 'a million bucks in it'. In addition, the witness claimed, Walter Bishop had his father Albert appear onstage at a barn dance with a chicken under his arm and had introduced him as Paw Kettle (although this allegation was later contradicted by another witness). In addition, a deposition from the editor of the *Port Townsend Leader* explained that he had published a story about the Bishop farm being the 'Kettle farm' because the Bishops' daughter Madeline had given him permission to print it. The Bishops, witnesses testified, had definitely promoted the story that they were the real-life Kettles in order to profit. This of course somewhat detracted from their complaints of ridicule and humiliation.

Then came Betty's turn on the stand. Her attorney George Guttormsen's strategy was to paint *Egg* as purely a work of fiction.

'Our testimony will show she kept no diary while living on the Peninsula,' he told the jurors. 'She had no records on which to base *The Egg and I*, and no file of letters on which to draw as material for the book. Not the smallest source of information was the Seattle Public Library, where she spent long periods of time acquiring historical background of the Olympic Peninsula and history of the Indians which she included in her book. Our testimony will bring out that there is no living character in the book as far as she is concerned. She did not depict anyone she knew.'

To prove his points to the court Guttormsen questioned Betty about the genesis of *Egg*.

'I had become very irritated by women who wrote books about living in the country without lights and running water and just loved it,' Betty replied. 'I thought I'd write the other side.'

Asked how often she had visited the Albert Bishop family, Betty said:

'Not very many times. We were friendly, but I didn't see them often.'

She stated that she had never attended the late Susanna Bishop's birthday party, that she had never seen Raymond Johnson before the suit hearing opened and that, as far as she knew, there were no persons named Geoduck, Clamface and Crowbar in real life. They were simply characters in the book.

When Guttormsen asked whether she had described the Bishop family as the Kettles, Betty replied:

'I did not.'

She stuck to her guns, denying that she had kept a diary, letters, or records of her four years on the Olympic Peninsula and insisting that the only living people depicted in her book were herself and members of her family. She had totally made up the book's settings and characters. Her sole intention in writing the book was to make fun of her own incompetence as a farm wife.

Press photographs showed Betty looking tired and drawn. Her old friend Blanche was following the case in the papers where she was teaching in Portland, Oregon, and wrote to offer her support. She knew that Betty loved people 'who do not fit into a set pattern' and she offered herself as a character witness willing to attest to this facet of Betty's nature.

Adding to the pressure on Betty, the trial was taking place during a period of terrible weather: heavy rains were causing flooding and landslides throughout the area of Puget Sound and there had been particularly heavy damage to Vashon Island. A slide at about 5:30 on the morning of 9 February had prevented Betty's appearance in court during the first half of the day. The slide had not touched Betty and Don's home, but it had marooned them and others along the beach by blocking the beach trail and the road leading out of their property; stuck in the house with Sydney, Anne, Anne's husband and their two tiny children, Betty had been unable to get away until about eleven when the tide had receded. Power and telephone lines had been torn down. A local newspaper reported that Betty and her family were marooned in their beach home beneath a slipping clay cliff which threatened at any time to smash down and engulf them, and that the MacDonalds were in sight of a neighbor's summer cottage which had been completely ruined by the pre-dawn avalanche. Another paper reported that Betty's own home had itself been damaged by a slide, and while this was not in fact the case, Betty's brother Cleve did report on 10 February that his sister's property, valued at between $50,000 and $60,000, was in grave danger. Luckily, the bad weather had retreated by the time Betty was undergoing her ordeal on the stand.

Closing arguments were presented on 19 February.

Plaintiff attorney Crandell argued that the immutable law of chance had been violated if it were just coincidence that Betty gave her book what he said were accurate descriptions of the Bishops and their home. The book's only recommendation was 'filth and slime' and it had cast a bad reflection on the Bishops as a 'wholesome pioneer family'.

Betty's attorney Guttormsen had carefully referred to the book as a novel throughout and had avoided any mention of the settlement of the first suit in 1949, since of course this was a compromise which might have suggested some acknowledgment of the claim of libel. Now he argued that locals had actually profited from *The Egg and I* rather than the reverse. He stated that there were highway signs posted near the farm where Betty had lived during the years she described. These signs had been posted by a relative of the Bishop family by marriage, Anita Larson, who was living there when the book was published; her signs directed visitors to the farm where she charged money to curious tourists to view Betty's old home, which the Larsons were using as a chicken house. A guest book was kept for the visitors which eventually contained the names of visitors from over sixty countries. Additionally, in 1946 a real estate notice in a local newspaper had advertised that '*The Egg and I* farm' was up for sale by the Larsons; the notice stated that along with the property came the opportunity to charge tourists an entrance fee of one dollar per car, and that this had already netted the Larsons over $500.

Guttormsen insisted that there could not possibly have been a connection between the book and the Bishops if these people had not deliberately come out and made that connection themselves. 'Is that Betty MacDonald's fault? The problems of the Bishop family spring from the things they've done, not what Betty has done.' His client had not begun writing her book until long after she had left her residence near the Bishop home. 'Can you tell me that she'd remember conversations so well as to characterize the Bishop family?' He also made the point that testimony during the trial brought out by the plaintiffs themselves made Johnson too young to be the Crowbar of the book.

Judge Wilkins' instructions to the jury took forty minutes. The court was full of spectators and a line of people were even waiting in the corridor in hopes of admittance. Wilkins told the jury that each of the ten cases was to be decided separately. If the jury found the plaintiffs had been libeled they were to recover only nominal damages, which he said could be one dollar or under, unless it had been established that they had 'suffered actual and substantial damage by the publication of the book'. In the judge's view libel was only deemed published if the reader personally knew the Bishops, which of course the bulk of Betty's millions of readers did not. Evidence of plaintiffs' identification with characters in the book was to be completely disregarded in the matter of the amount of damages, if any, awarded. Further, no plaintiff could be awarded damages if he or she had tried to profit from the identification.

He also instructed the members of the jury to consider the book in its entirety. In a literal interpretation of these instructions the jury accordingly read the entire book aloud as they considered their verdict, which altogether took them twenty-four hours. Jurors were then polled individually on each of the ten cases, Bishops plus Johnson, and each agreed that none of the plaintiffs could be identified as a character in the book. The decision was therefore unanimously in favor of the defendants. Betty had won.

She was not in court as she had not expected the verdict to come so quickly; she was at Mary's where she had been staying since the slides the previous week. Don was present, however, and thanked the jury. Betty's stated reaction, unsurprisingly, was that she was very, very happy. **BETTY WINS** blazed the headline in the *Seattle Post-Intelligencer*. She told the newspaper that she had spent the day anxiously drinking cup after cup of coffee and going crazy. As regards the verdict, her comment was that

If the decision had been adverse, it might be possible for anyone to squeeze themselves into any book – I have had letters from people from all over the world – from England to Bavaria – telling me that the Kettles lived next door to them. I even had a letter from a woman who said Mrs. Kettle was her mother-in-law. She lived in Florida.

Her only comfort during the two-week trial, she continued, had been the realization that she could be a good enough writer to have people identify themselves with her books.

When it was all over, Betty wrote to every single juror, thanking them fervently for the verdict and commiserating with them for having to sit for so long on such hard seats, listening to the same bits from *Egg* read out over and over. She could only hope, she said, that if she were ever sued again it would be for a different book.

As for Bud Bishop, the grandson who had helped Betty and the girls keep warm by cutting wood for them, there was at least one consolation. Betty, so far as the law was concerned, was declared to have invented what seemed to him to be untruthful and demeaning descriptions of his family's hardscrabble lives. To his mind, no one had done more for Betty in her hour of need than the Bishops.

§

Given the hundreds of thousands in damages sought by the plaintiffs, the suit had certainly represented a serious threat to Betty and her publishers. Nevertheless, right from the start the trial had assumed a comical tone, and Seattle newspapers had happily milked the comic aspects with daily coverage. The plaintiffs, the supporting witnesses and their statements were colorful. The elderly widow Annie McGuire, looking like a lumberjack in a black and red checked shirt, could not contain her own laughter when passages from the book were read to her but still insisted that she would have 'beat up' Betty at the time of the book's publication had she been able to find her. Forty-year-old mechanic Wilbur Bishop, who claimed to be the model for the teenaged Elwin Kettle, thrust his face towards each juror to let them judge whether or not he had the blue eyes ascribed to Elwin in the book (he did). This performance provoked 'appreciative laughter' in the courtroom. More amusement was derived from the discrepancy between the number of children in the Bishop family, thirteen, and the fact that there were fifteen in the supposedly fictional Kettle clan.

Some witnesses also misunderstood that the requirement was to show how similar the Bishops were to the Kettles, and instead pointed to the differences between certain upstanding Bishops and the ramshackle Kettle characters. The Bishops' daughter Madeline said that her late mother Susanna Bishop was clearly Ma Kettle but then went on that her mother had never used profanity, unlike Ma Kettle, whose speech was liberally laced with obscenities. Susanna's brother said that Susanna didn't have time to be 'primping herself up' but that she was generally neat in appearance and not a slattern like Ma in

Egg. Albert Bishop himself, the brother said, was 'clean, in every way that I know of'. One witness carefully explained that Betty's description of Pa Kettle's business as 'begging' did not really fit Albert Bishop, who in the opinion of the witness was 'not lazy, perhaps a bit impractical'. Other witnesses failed to understand that the Bishops were claiming they had suffered as a result of *Egg*: some former neighbors testified that their regard for the Bishops was unchanged, despite the book. Testimony like this actually bolstered Betty's defense.

Comic as the trial may have been in parts, and despite acquittal, the question remains as to Betty's credibility in arguing that *The Egg and I* was nothing but make-believe or composites. Her note to her publishers in about 1945 had admitted that the Kettles were based on the Bishops. Her use of 'Docktown' and 'Town' as names cannot obscure the striking similarities between her descriptions and the actual towns of Port Ludlow and Port Townsend. The book's vivid descriptions of Docktown's sawmill and company store, and of Town's red stone courthouse, Victorian houses, army post, and long sweeping hill curving down to the harbor can hardly be coincidental. A woman witness who formerly lived near Port Ludlow had insisted that 'Docktown' was a perfect description of Port Ludlow. Of 'Town' in the book she declared, 'It's Port Townsend.' The Kettles may not have been exclusively based on the Bishops but the similar size of the real and fictional families, the way they lived their lives, and incidents like the burning down of the barn indicate definite parallels. Betty herself, in a Hollywood interview in 1946, admitted that Pa Kettle would be immediately recognizable as the original (adding that he wouldn't care).

Betty's daughter Joan later stated that the lawsuit was one of the biggest challenges Betty ever had to face. Her mother had wanted to make a statement that authors could write stories using composite characters without being sued by people claiming to be those characters, she said, but at the same time conceding that some of the people that testified really did look and act like Ma and Pa Kettle. During her cross-examination Betty did admit, 'Every book is based to some extent on facts, or else how could you write?'

She certainly appears to have misled the jury about one crucial fact. In a 1949 essay on Betty's mother Sydney, the Seattle writer and family friend Margaret Bundy Callahan included Sydney's innocent comment that Betty *was* in the habit of keeping a diary while on the farm. If so, Betty is more than likely to have kept it and to have referred to it in writing *Egg*. Betty also wrote in a letter to a fan in 1945 – again, years before any thought of a lawsuit – that Port Townsend was indeed the 'Town' referred to. Did Betty flee the courtroom because she knew she wasn't being entirely truthful?

The judge had the last word. When the trial was over, the plaintiffs immediately launched an appeal to have the jury's verdict overruled. Judge Wilkins denied their motion for a new trial but accompanied that decision with some interesting comments. He declared that if the lawsuit had been tried before him without a jury he 'might have allowed nominal damages to several of the plaintiffs and perhaps, in some cases, even more'. However, the difference between the interpretation that he made of the evidence and that made by the jury was not so overwhelming that he could justify overruling the verdict. Had he himself been on the jury, Judge Wilkins continued, he might have at least concluded that the author had the individuals and their traits in mind when writing the book, though it could be said that elements of the descriptions were fictional. 'The jury, however, found otherwise.'

In his 1981 autobiography, Judge Wilkins wrote that 'attractive, auburn-haired' Betty had been a very convincing witness.

Perhaps too convincing.

Bob Heskett

BOB HESKETT, Betty's first husband, had not prospered after their divorce. He never remarried. Not long after Betty left he sold the farm, moved back to Seattle and returned to selling insurance for the Mutual Life Insurance Company. By 1942, when he was forty-six years old, Bob was living in Oakland, California, in a modest neighborhood close to the waterfront and rail yards, working as a carpenter and listed as a member of the local carpenters' union. He registered for the draft that same year, giving his employer as the Southern Pacific railroad company, but with his medical discharge record Bob was unlikely to have served again. He never benefited from the success of *The Egg and I*.

In July 1951, when Bob was fifty-five and still living in Oakland, a woman moved in with him. Thelma Blake was twenty years younger than Bob, and her two young daughters, aged five and seven, moved in also. Perhaps there was some draw there for Bob, some reminder of his own lost daughters.

A week after Thelma came to live with Bob, her ex-husband Thomas J. Blake, a bulldozer driver, turned up at about midnight and demanded to see Thelma and his 'babies'. Bob asked Blake to leave but he refused to go and a fight ensued. As the two grappled in a hallway, Bob suddenly toppled over a banister: he had been fatally stabbed in the heart by Blake. The following day Blake was charged with Bob's murder, which he claimed had been in self-defense. According to Blake he didn't wield the knife until Bob swung at him with a hatchet, a claim that was contradicted by Thelma, who had witnessed the fight.

In October Blake pleaded guilty to manslaughter. The District Attorney's office had agreed to the lesser charge after investigation showed that the two had fought before the stabbing. On 30 October Blake was sentenced to one to ten years in San Quentin prison.

Bob was buried on 8 August in Golden Gate National Cemetery in San Bruno, California. Betty's reaction to the shocking murder of her first husband and the father of her children is not known. Newspapers described her as 'unavailable for comment'.

The death of Bob Heskett meant that Don could finally file for adoption of Anne and Joan, despite the fact that both were now adults and using their married names. The adoption was finalized that same year, Joan taking the opportunity to change her middle name from Dorothy (after Bob's sister) to Sydney, and Anne adding Campbell as a new middle name.

The Hesketts were an unlucky family. There are reports that Bob's sister Katherine drowned when she was in her twenties; his youngest sister Dorothy's first husband also drowned. Bob's father Otis, a witness at Bob and Betty's wedding, died after a car crash in 1940.

Betty and California

BETTY'S next book for children, *Nancy and Plum*, was published in 1952. When Betty told Anne and Joan the old stories she used to tell Mary in bed at night when they were little, Joan became Plum and Anne was Nancy. Blanche remembered Betty making it up as she went along, asking them each where she had left off; the girls would say, 'Well, it was where Plum put the fish bowl on Marybell Whistle's head,' or 'where Mrs. Monday made Nancy and Plum do all the dishes.' The story is about two orphan girls whose rich uncle sends them away to a terrible boarding school run by the evil Mrs. Monday. The orphans are fed cold, hard oatmeal and any presents sent to them are taken away and given to Mrs. Monday's niece Marybell. Finally, Nancy and Plum (short for Pamela) find a way to send a letter out – by chicken – and after many adventures Mrs. Monday is sent to jail, the girls send fabulous presents to all their friends and at last find a wonderful family to live with. Both *Mrs. Piggle-Wiggle* and *Nancy and Plum* were made into very successful plays by the Seattle Children's Theater, and the celebrated children's author Jacqueline Wilson has said that *Nancy and Plum* is her favorite children's book. However, Lippincott were unenthusiastic about *Nancy and Plum* and neither they nor Betty's agent Bernice encouraged her to launch a series, despite a trove of previously told tales waiting to be written up.

To some extent Betty was feeling left behind. Other Seattle writers were being talked about and she was not, she complained sadly to her daughter Joan. Feeling unappreciated was part of Betty and Don's decision to move away from Seattle. In June 1952, after some months of searching, they bought ranch land in California's Carmel Valley with the intention of raising cattle. No doubt both also wanted a quiet life after so many hectic years of fanfare and public appearances. There was the added attraction of constant sunshine: when asked if she was moving because she disliked the Pacific Northwest, Betty responded that she loved the Pacific Northwest but that California had ten months of sun and only two of rain. And, as she was a writer, 'new scenes are indicated'.

Their new home in Monterey County, the Corral de Tierra Ranch, was a 2,000-acre spread on top of a steep incline, a property of rolling hills and huge oaks from which they could see valleys, mountains, eleven towns and even the Pacific Ocean (when it wasn't foggy, Betty admitted). There was a small house and a barn on the property, which came with 222 Hereford cattle and five saddle horses which Betty intended to learn to ride – a neighbor, a friend of the legendary movie cowboy Will Rogers, promised to teach her in two days. As the move began she and Don eagerly looked forward to their new life, even if a friend did immediately send them a report predicting a black future for the cattle business. Their future neighbors in Monterey County awaited the final arrival of the new owners with interest: Betty was still very famous, and they were curious as to how the MacDonalds would manage such a large ranch.

It had been acquired with no down payment. Betty and Don had no savings, despite the huge amount of money that had rolled in from Betty's books and advertising deals. Both had assumed that they would easily be able to sell all their property in Washington State – their home on Vashon, the adjacent barn property, and the Howe St.

house – and thus be able to meet their new mortgage payments. But despite listing the Vashon home nationally, and making much of its famous owners with enticing photographs showing Betty on the patio and digging clams on the beach with Don, the property did not sell. Don went ahead to manage matters in California while Betty was forced to stay behind and try and sell the homes, writing when she could and helping out with the grandchildren and her daughters' pregnancies.

The Howe St. house finally sold but Betty and Sydney remained stuck on Vashon, trying to maintain the place in good order for potential buyers. When Don was not visiting from California, Betty felt isolated. She was still unable to drive and the little town of Vashon was not within walking distance. Eventually she took driving lessons and passed her test in late 1953, but felt too lacking in confidence to drive at night until many years later.

In early February 1954, still on Vashon, Betty wrote her old friend Bertram Lippincott, who by then had retired from publishing, that he would love the ranch. It was beautiful, she told him, if not yet exactly what you would call profitable. She said she was chained to her typewriter trying to finish a new book by the end of the month. She had only just started it and was using the title *Onions in the Stew* but it was another 'I' book, as she put it, this time about the island they had lived on for so many years. 'I think I'm being pretty funny but may be only hysterical – a state not helped by the Republican Party – '. Betty continued that Anne and her second husband Bob Evans were expecting a baby and were due to leave for Sun Valley for two weeks. Normally she would have had the children for them, but this time she had said no because she had to write at least one book for Lippincott's that year. She told her old friend that she no longer felt that she had the rapport with the company that she used to have when he was still there, and invited Bert and his wife to come for a visit on her birthday in March so they could all get drunk and 'maudlinly sentimental'.

When Don did visit, some of Betty's occasional impatience would surface. 'Though I adore him I get a hell of a lot more done when he is not here,' she wrote to Bernice about a writing deadline. But, landed sometimes with too many guests or children to look after, Betty also felt annoyed when she pictured Don enjoying life in the sunshine. Writing to him in April 1954 she asked how he would feel if she really did stop her writing – which 'God knows' she wanted to do – and how many people would suddenly have to take care of themselves. Perhaps referring to his willingness to be apart, or to let her shoulder the burdens, she continued,

I honestly think, Don, that that ranch has ruined any chances we might have had for happiness because it showed me how you really feel about me – actions do speak louder than words, you know.

As spring of 1954 turned into summer Betty began to feel desperate. Don was still in California, although not living on the ranch, and the latest calf crop had turned out well below what they had counted on for money. She struggled on, staying up at night to watch the McCarthy communism hearings on TV and worrying about finances. She asked Bernice how much money she might hope for from another *Mrs. Piggle-Wiggle* book, which would be less of a grind to write. 'I want all I can get,' Betty stressed.

In all, Betty was to remain a full three years on Vashon without Don, only occasionally traveling to visit him in Carmel Valley. She still managed to write, though (even including work on a TV script), and *Onions in the Stew* was published early in 1955. She had worked hard to get the book out, needing to pay back the advance of ten thousand dollars she had long before received – and spent - from Lippincott. An early version, a novel, had been jettisoned. She had wanted to write fiction again, as she had done with her early short stories, and to escape using her own life in her books; after three autobiographical works, Betty yearned to try something new. For a period of two years she wove a tale about a group of characters stranded in a remote coastal motel during a storm, just as she herself was stranded on Vashon. But Betty's agent Bernice Baumgarten thought the work needed more dramatic action, and asked for a rewrite.

Completely dashed, Betty could not afford the time to revise her manuscript. More money was needed, and fast. She suggested a cook book followed by a gardening book, the first perhaps to be called *The Stove and I* – not that she liked the title, she told Bernice, it made her retch, but people expected it. Again Bernice was averse, and instead asked Lippincott if they would be willing to accept another autobiographical work. The publisher agreed, and thus Betty was forced into her fourth and final 'I' book.

She at least retained the title of her painfully abandoned novel, *Onions in the Stew*, which came from the poet Charles Divine's poem about a café in Greenwich Village, *At the Lavender Lantern*:

Where hearts were high, and fortunes low, and onions in the stew

Betty's language in the new book, once completed, again caused a few raised eyebrows. A Lippincott editor worried that the swearing and frankness might alienate a more Puritanical 1950s readership, and expressed reservations about 'the Goddamns, the Jesuses and the passage towards the end about adolescent discovery of sex': in his eyes the likeability of Betty's family and the readers' probable identification with them constituted the chief draw of *Onions*, and stood to be harmed by the franker inclusions. He worried, too, about the possibility of libel, and insisted that for characters other than Betty's family, names and identifying features must be changed. Betty assured him that many of the characters were either made up or composites. She stated that her description in the book of the luscious 'Lesley Arnold', with whom Don in *Onions* spends a summer flirting, was not at all like the original, who in Betty's eyes ought to be flattered. But she uncomplainingly toned down all the colorful language.

The book's unsentimental account of Betty's life on Vashon with her family in the early to mid 1940s is just as much fun as her other books, if not usually listed as the fans' favorite. As in *Egg*, there are lyrical descriptions of the beautiful Northwest. Oval ponds lie in green fields 'like forgotten handmirrors', 'green dance-hall streamers of boysenberry' loop from post to post and strawberry patches roll up to the edge of the sky, the troughs between each one 'scalloping the horizon'. And, across the Sound,

...every evening dark red and orange freighters glide toward the Strait; their booms fore and aft, picked out by the late sunshine, look like Tinker Toys. Filmy scarves of gray smoke trail behind them, a heavy wake thunders in to shore after they are out of sight. At night or in the early morning we hear the chunk, chunk, chunk of tugs no bigger than chips, huffing and puffing as they drag huge fantails of logs to the mills.

The *New York Times* review likened Betty to Mark Twain, while *Newsweek* called Betty's humor in the book 'tigerish' and even 'sadistic', although for the most part it is far milder than her previous works and the content more domestic, no doubt reflecting the happy early days of her second marriage. Far more mercy is shown to eccentric neighbors than was the case in *Egg*, or than was shown to fellow patients and nurses in her account of life in a tuberculosis sanatorium. Perhaps as a consequence, the *Saturday Review* wrote that *Onions* never quite achieves the 'bubbling hilarity' of *The Egg and I*, but that readers would put down the book thinking how much they would like to know Betty MacDonald. Her writing was the projection of a remarkably attractive personality, the review declared, with Betty managing to sound relaxed and friendly and just like anybody else. However, the reviewer continued, readers should also realize that only a writer of uncommon talent and considerable sensitivity could create so winning an impression of naturalness.

Onions sold twenty-six thousand copies in the first month alone, becoming the *New York Times'* Book-of-the-Month dual choice in June 1955 and finding a place on the newspaper's list of Outstanding Books of the Year. When it hit the book stands in London, the figures were even higher: sixty-four thousand copies in less than a month. In 1956 there was a television show based on the book starring Constance Bennett, and it was also adapted into a stage play which focused on the book's content about Anne and Joan's protracted adolescence. The piece became a favorite for high-school performances. (Betty dedicated the book to 'Joan and Jerry and Anne and Bob – our best friends'.)

Betty had finally joined Don in California in early 1955, and she returned to Seattle for Lippincott's launch of the book at the Washington Athletic Club on 18 May. In reference to the book's title, white Bermuda onions had been placed among the flowers at all the tables and Betty, Anne and Joan each held a couple as they posed for the cameras. Perhaps having learned the lesson from the sluggish sales of *Anybody*, Betty also agreed to promote her new book with a number of book signing events while in the city. Her appearance at Frederick & Nelson's department store sold 340 copies, the most successful signing session in the store's history.

Courtesy Seattle's Museum of History and Industry

The Vashon house had been rented out. In August 1956, still on the market, it was advertised for sale in the *Seattle Times* as Home of the Year. 'Picture yourself owning the (dream) home described in *Onions in the Stew*,' the ad urged. Betty's beloved beach house, going at $39,500, was described as a low, rambling sandstone and timber home with 200 ft. of sandy beach and a salt waterfront, within walking distance of Vashon Island ferry. According to the ad about $100,000 had been spent on rebuilding in 1948.

The description of the living space mentioned the 40-ft living room with floors of pegged, planked pine and the enormous stone fireplace that Betty had talked about in *Onions*, but also the new, spacious guest house built by Betty and Don. Instructions for the Open Day viewings included where to drop hook if you came by boat.

Betty, Don and Sydney were now finally settled in Monterey. Sydney would sometimes go off to stay with one of her other children, but for the most part she remained on the ranch with Betty. With the Vashon property still unsold, the proceeds from the sale of the Howe St. house had been insufficient to build the large home they had dreamed of, and the three had to make do with the small house already on the property. There were other problems. Water was short on the ranch and watering their cattle from the two wells and two springs, which were far from the house and often ran dry, had to take precedence over washing and watering their garden. Betty and Don dug several new wells, but without success.

From their new abode Betty wrote to Blanche in January 1956 about the rickety old house they were living in and the constant rain and minor hurricanes which kept them busy repairing damage. She talked about their attempt to find a cattle dog for Don and how she was dying to get a Great Dane and a Boxer from a pet adopting agency, but Don said she was always needlessly complicating her life. Nevertheless, they ended up not only with dogs but several big cats and lots of kittens, and Betty said she spent hours each week cooking and distributing oatmeal and milk. They had hired a Russian, Alex, to help Don build some bookcases. Alex, who spoke no English, had been brought over by the Government to work in a language school but then let go, and Betty clearly felt sorry for him as an exile widowed with four small children and unable to get a job without US citizenship. She reported to Blanche that Don got angry when there were communication difficulties and talked to the Russian in a 'big loud bossy voice'. To make up for it, Betty said, she played Rachmaninoff records and make Alex big hot lunches.

Although Democrats, their new social life in California also included 'millionaire Republican parties' (perhaps for reasons of diplomacy) which Betty said bored her to tears. In typical Betty style she described one of her hostesses as

...small and brown and grasping with tiny little darting eyes – she uses lots of little dirty expressions and there is lots of what we in our family call 'peepee talk' among them all with much cheap laughter and corny remarks because Don and I have been marooned up here on the ranch – 'bet you were busy' they say nudging each other and looking cheap.

Betty's letter-writing style is idiosyncratic, dashes in place of punctuation, racing on with plenty of jokes and character assassination. Of a cocktail party 'for about 150 old Admirals and Generals' she wrote that she hadn't had her behind stroked or pinched so much in years. There was plenty to stroke and pinch too, she added, as she had been meaning to go on a starvation diet but kept testing out new recipes. Clearly Betty still retained her interest in good food.

After being with all those rich Republicans Betty told Blanche she could hardly wait to get back to their cozy little ranch house and her 'easy sloppy <u>bright</u> Democratic friends'. The rich Republican crowd traveled in clusters, she wrote: first they all went to Mexico, then they all went to Europe, then Aspen, then the Hawaiian Islands. They all looked alike and dressed alike and she would have said 'thought alike', except that in Betty's opinion they didn't think. On her own side of the political fence, a Democrat acquaintance invited them to join the Monterey branch of the London Wine and Food Society – which she knew would be dull but possibly material for an article for the *New Yorker* – because Betty was Honorary Chairman of the Stevenson for President Committee. (Democrat Adlai Stevenson ran against incumbent president Dwight D. Eisenhower in the 1956 US Presidential Election but was defeated.) She joked to Blanche that she hid from Don the fact that drinking cocktails and smoking were not allowed at the Society meetings.

A few years earlier she had reported Don as very content with his new life as a cattle rancher and happier than she had ever known him, 'very brown and very handsome and very sweet'. Don became a member of the Carmel Valley Horsemen's Association, taking part in local roundups and holding barbecues with Betty for fellow members who had assisted with the roundups at their own Corral de Tierra ranch. She, too, was in love with the ranch, she had written at that point to Joan and Jerry. She adored it and never wanted to live anywhere else; everybody was proud to have her living nearby and the two local bookstores were stocking all her books. She liked their new neighbors, whom she described as mostly intellectuals and good cooks who entertained in true Sydney style: 'lots of dust under the bed but beautiful flower arrangements'.

But as time went on Betty began to feel more unhappy with Don. Some of the earlier honeymoon bliss Betty had felt on the ranch, both in the early days of the move and once she had joined Don there permanently, had evaporated. She felt more and more frustrated with him;

he was 'Bishopy', she told her family, meaning lazy and bad-tempered like her old neighbors on the chicken ranch.

Sydney

While Betty and Don were getting to grips with their new life Betty's mother Sydney, previously in vigorous health, was starting to fade. In a 1954 article about her mother for *Reader's Digest*, Betty wrote that a friend had recently watched Sydney wheel a heavy barrow of chicken manure down the garden at Vashon, dump it out, rake it vigorously around the rose bushes and then take off her gardening gloves and light a cigarette. The friend had sighed how lucky Betty was to have such a young mother and Betty had looked at her in amazement. Sydney was then seventy-five but erect and slender, tanned and serene. But by her late seventies, long troubled by a constant cough from smoking her Camels, Sydney began to experience heart problems. She had one severe heart attack and then another when Joan and Jerry were holidaying at the ranch. After the second attack the doctor told Betty that Sydney could not possibly live through the night but that if by some miracle she did, she would undoubtedly live another twenty years. Sydney did survive and later said she felt remarkably well, if driven insane by being unable to do much. This she took with her usual grace, although occasionally irritable. But after another short illness she was taken to a Monterey hospital and died in August 1957 at the age of seventy-nine.

Betty and Don had been to see her in the hospital early that same evening and Sydney had been feeling quite well, so the visit was an enjoyable one. She was sitting up in bed reading the *Saturday Evening Post* and complaining about the hideous décor of her room, Betty wrote a friend. Over the past year, despite her increasing frailty she had become mentally sharper and sharper, said Betty, and was still reading numerous magazines and a book a day (and had almost given up smoking). On the way home Betty and Don stopped at a lookout to watch the sun slowly disappear in a magnificent sunset. They both felt it had been a spiritual experience and neither said a word the rest of the way home. As they entered the house the hospital called to say that Sydney had died a few minutes before, just as they were watching the sun go down.

Betty dedicated one of her *Mrs Piggle-Wiggle* books to her mother and she had provided many loving glimpses of calm, wise Sydney in her other books. Sydney had made her home with Betty and Don for many years, somewhere to keep her most precious possessions – her pictures of Darsie, her sewing box and her sketching things. But she also made regular visits to her brother, Jim Sanderson, or went where she was needed most in the family, often looking after her grandchildren while their parents were away. Each of her other three daughters and her son had a room in the house for Sydney to come and stay, which the grandchildren always enjoyed. She had a calm, commanding presence and the children knew they had to behave well and obey her quietly spoken orders, but she was also greatly loved. She cooked delicious meals, patiently taught them to paint and draw, and listened with real interest to their stories about school and friends. Sydney never scolded or criticized or gave unsolicited advice. Just as she had done in Betty's childhood, she allowed her grandchildren to play hooky from school if they had what she considered a valid reason (such as wanting to listen to a soap opera on the radio or finish a good book). She was particular about what constituted a good book, but would make no comment as she made cookies and milk for whoever was staying home to sniffle along to corny dramas like *Stella Dallas*.

When she was with Betty and Don on Vashon, Sydney would help with Betty's fan mail, do most of the gardening, take care of the house when Betty was writing, make lovely water-color and pastel sketches of the beautiful Puget Sound country, cook for umpteen people, help babysit Betty's grandchildren, give Betty moral support when her writing flagged, make exquisite flower arrangements, and read constantly. In summer she and Betty would go swimming at least once a day in the icy waters of the Sound, plowing through the waves down to the end of their sea wall and back, about 400 feet each way. Sydney swam breaststroke, despite Betty's efforts to teach her the crawl, because she said she liked to see where she was going. Afterwards they might build a bonfire on the beach and bake a salmon, and when the moon came up, sing songs as they cast for silvers in the incoming tide. Sydney would stay up late, even later than Betty, reading and reading. Dickens was a favorite, along with her perennial Galsworthys and Angela Thirkells.

Sydney made Christmases special. She would read traditional old stories aloud to the grandchildren: *Tiny Tim*, *The Night Before Christmas*, *The Little Christmas Tree*, *The Sugar Plum Tree*. She had long ago carefully divided up all the Bards' ancient Christmas ornaments, probably when she sold the much loved family home on 15th Avenue. To Mary as the eldest she had given the little Christmas tree that revolved as it played *Tannenbaum*, while the little birds with the spun-glass tails and all the other ornaments long ago inherited from her own family had been scrupulously allotted so that each of her children would have something. These little baubles, brought out year after year, would prompt memories of Christmases past: to Mary they would bring back Christmas Eves as a little girl in Butte, lying next to Betty in their shared bed. From outside would come the sound of the bells and the creaky runners of the sleighs in the snow, while from the next room came whispering and rustling as Sydney wrapped the children's presents with her handsome, beloved Darsie.

In Betty's view Sydney's serenity came from her refusal to feel sorry for herself. She had never indulged in the 'debilitating business of self-pity', Betty wrote in the article for *Reader's Digest*. Despite the terrible blow of Darsie's death, Betty could only remember Sydney expressing gratitude for the wonderful years she and Darsie had had together. When she lost all her money as a widow, through poor investments and bad advice, she didn't complain or become bitter. As the daughter of a wealthy and cultured family she had been brought up to believe that all nice people had enough money but also that money, like sex, was the man's responsibility; she had no head for finance herself. Instead of brooding over what was lost she simply worked hard at bringing up her five children and even several adopted ones like Madge Baldwin, who lived with the family for years. She added to the family income with her long-running radio serial *Schuyler Square.* Saddos are bores, Sydney would comment to her children. Nobody liked saddos. If you started to feel sorry for yourself, *do something!* Work in the garden, wash the windows, bake a pie, write a letter, anything. You couldn't be busy and sorry for yourself at the same time. Betty didn't know where Sydney had learned this secret of serenity but it had made her strenuous life a happy one. She wrote that Sydney was an enthusiastic and successful gardener, a superb cook, a talented artist, a first-rate fly fisherman, an excellent horsewoman. Those visits to her grandchildren were often more in the nature of a nursing service; she would arrive with the small brown suitcase she used exclusively for these trips and dispense calm and cheer in whatever crisis. She actually seemed to emanate a visible aura of peace, Betty observed. Sydney described this as just long practice in the face of disaster, but for Betty it was an inner serenity flowing from selflessness.

Sydney had taught her children strong values and how to feel good about themselves, despite the family having so little after Darsie's death. Her declared philosophy was to enjoy each day of living as it came along. She knew how to create an elegant environment, and how little things like lighting candles at dinner and a touch of lipstick could make all the difference. Her artistic talent and warmth was her legacy to her family; her love of good literature and intense interest in her fellow human beings her particular legacy to Betty.

Betty used the word 'spiritual' to describe what she and Don had felt watching the sunset, an unusual choice of word for Betty. Her grief at Sydney's death can be imagined.

Illness

Betty's next book was to have been *Too Old To Ride*, an account of her relationship with her beautiful sorrel horse, whose mane, she felt, was the color of her own hair. Ill health intervened.

She was suffering from an intensely irritating skin condition, an itch which drove her nearly demented. When it was particularly bad she would spend hours in the bath in an effort to get some relief. She tried allergists and even self-hypnosis, to no avail. Doctors suggested that the condition was psychosomatic, and with the lack of any obvious cause Betty felt ashamed of her troubles and rarely mentioned the itching even in letters to her family. Nevertheless, it was acute enough to prevent her writing.

Then, in late July 1955, came a visit back to Seattle to make a speech at a convention of insurance agents – a trip made reluctantly, as Betty disliked public speaking, but money was still short. She had spent her most recent advance from Lippincott, and she and Don were relying on her unpredictable royalty payments both for everyday living and to meet mortgage payments on their properties. While in Seattle Betty started to hemorrhage, and was sent to hospital for curettage. Her physician was concerned about the possibility of uterine cancer, but nothing was found. She returned to California, making another visit to Seattle that fall to help Anne with the children as her daughter waited to give birth for the fourth time.

When in Seattle she continued to consult her doctors, and in August 1956 she was diagnosed with probable endometriosis and scheduled for surgery. During the operation it finally became clear that Betty, a heavy smoker all her adult life, was suffering from advanced and inoperable ovarian cancer. Her doctors believed she might die within a matter of weeks.

At Don's request, she was not told of the diagnosis for ten days after the surgery. She would rather not have been told at all. As she later wrote to her agent Bernice,

I still can't see the good of telling a person they have cancer – I would have been so happy with endometriosis or whatever it was and I'm not sure I'm enough of a Pollyanna to go whistling through life with a huge axe on the back of my neck.

After leaving the hospital Betty stayed at Mary's while she underwent two months of radiation treatment. On returning to Carmel Valley she still felt tired, but slowly became stronger. She told Bernice that Don waited on her hand and foot like a saint, and was very patient with her natural feelings of depression, try as she might to fight against them. Her state of mind and physical health were not helped by having to cope with Sydney's last days. Despite her own ills Betty nevertheless managed to fly her mother to Seattle for family visits in December 1956, getting help at the various airports with Sydney in her wheelchair.

For Americans in the 1950s there was no diagnosis of illness more dreaded than cancer. Heart disease killed twice as many people annually, but malignant tumors were more greatly feared. In 1954, when Mary's doctor husband Clyde Jensen was a member of the American Cancer Society's state executive board and chairman of the Washington State Medical Society's neoplastic committee (neoplasm meaning the growth of abnormal tissue), he had been one of a number of doctors in Seattle's King County who became concerned about the need for early cancer detection. Together these medics developed a nine-point cancer check-up program for local doctors to sign up to, which they did in their hundreds. By 1957 the benefits of smear (pap) testing were also becoming more widely known. Betty may well have felt the benefit of having Clyde in her corner, and that her Seattle doctors were providing better care generally. The itching and tiredness which had plagued her for five long years, dismissed by her California doctors as psychosomatic, were revealed to be caused by a foreign protein produced by the cancer. She nevertheless promised to have her condition monitored by cancer specialists in her new home state.

A fifth *Mrs. Piggle-Wiggle* book was still due to Lippincott but naturally Betty struggled to get down to it. As she regained some strength she took pleasure in the beauties of the ranch, taking long walks to soak up the vibrant colors of the many flowers she had planted in her garden and the more muted tones of California's native chaparral and sage. She wrote lyrically to Anne of the singing birds and cloudless sky and all she could see around her. Mary visited for three weeks in the spring of 1957 and, wandering through fields of wildflowers, she and Betty reminisced about their childhood.

The old tensions with Don seemed to have fallen away, Mary noted in correspondence, and she took pains to overcome her old reserve about her sister's husband. As she had always done, she jollied Betty along and encouraged her to get started on her projected book about life on the ranch, *Too Old to Ride*. But Mary knew that underneath it all Betty was living in fear.

Betty recognized how good Mary's practicality was for her, and also that she still needed to earn money. She was $5000 in debt to Lippincott for their advance for the next *Mrs. Piggle-Wiggle* book and finally got down to work, at the same time trying to complete an outline for the ranch book in order to secure another advance of $25,000. Lippincott cold-bloodedly demanded a doctor's guarantee that she would not die before completion. 'I'm certainly going to have type faster than I've been doing,' Betty wrote drily to Bernice.

But the itching continued to plague her, and she was also suffering from what she believed to be gallbladder attacks, for which she avoided animal fats and took atropine and Epsom salts before every meal. The attacks were depressing and exhausting. A month of bad back pain took her to her California gynecologist, who assured her that the tumor they were monitoring was very small and that she was fine. Betty was not impressed with the care, telling Mary that the Seattle doctors were one billion percent better.

She soldiered on, hosting a visit from Anne and her family in June with trips to Carmel Village for shopping and to the beach. Sydney's death came in August, reported both locally and more widely by the Associated Press wire service. Appearing in print as the mother of Betty MacDonald, Sydney had become as celebrated as her daughter.

§

Very soon after Sydney's death Betty's carcinoma was found to have returned. Just prior to a visit to Seattle her California doctor had told her she was in fine condition, but her true state was revealed on examination by the doctors in Seattle. Further radiation was ordered and Betty found herself once again undergoing treatment at the private Maynard Hospital on Summit Avenue, where her brother-in-law Clyde was an attending physician (and where her daughter Joan's first child had been born in 1951).

When not in the hospital Betty as usual stayed at Mary's, who observed in a letter that Betty was slowly adjusting to the idea that she was possibly facing death. The family's old friend Margaret Bundy Callaghan visited and could see that the Bards were seriously thrown by Betty's illness but were not allowing it to depress them. Apart from wiping her eyes a few times Betty herself seemed to Margaret completely the same as usual, although 'thin and showing the results of the surgery and the bad news'. Betty's former schoolmate Blanche likewise went to Mary's to see her old friend. The household was busy as Mary got her three daughters off to school and, practically for the first time in her life, Blanche found Betty feeling sorry for herself and unable to make a joke of her problems in her usual way. She told Blanche she was a big saddo and that Mary and her family were all so busy she wondered if they even knew she was in the house. She and Blanche chatted and tried to be 'old be-happies' but to Blanche it rang hollow.

Betty's old friend, the painter William Cumming, commented in his memoir that he had heard Betty was bitter about her illness because she believed the danger of cancer could have been picked up at the time of her gynecological surgery in the 1940s. She wrote to a Lippincott editor in early December that the past few months had been 'really gruesome', in fact the worst of her entire life. She was as thin as a thread, she told him, and expected to get even thinner due to the constant nausea. She could only write by taking two codeine, waiting twenty minutes for them to take effect and then writing madly before she began to gag – 'this of course without any pause for thought, wit or clever phrasing.'

One day the phone rang at Blanche's. It was Betty at the Maynard: she wanted Blanche to bring her a bologna sandwich with plenty of mustard. Blanche rushed to make the sandwich and take it to Betty, whom she found in fine fettle and delighted to get her snack. During the visit a nurse came in to announce that a couple from Chile were downstairs and that the wife wanted to meet Betty, who was her favorite author. Betty cheerfully complied and chatted happily to her fan, first introducing Blanche as her best friend. Blanche was flattered. She felt the woman's visit was joyful and touching, and all three ended by exchanging addresses.

Radiation was finally discontinued and Betty entered the Maynard for the last time just before Christmas 1957. Nothing further could be done, and she was given palliative care in a private room.

A Christmas card arrived for Blanche from the woman in Chile and Blanche called Betty at the hospital to check if she had received one too. But Betty was not as alert and sparkly as usual; it was obvious that she was under sedation. She said, 'Blanchie, shame on you. Here I am on my deathbed, and you're out there stealing my friends!'

They both laughed and said good-bye. It was to be the last time that Blanche joked with her old friend.

Don clung to the last shreds of hope and wrote to Bernice Baumgarten in February 1958 that he still thought she might improve, and that he had asked her to hold on and she was trying. Betty was the bravest person that ever lived, he wrote.

News of Betty's illness broke in the press on 6 February and letters began to pour in from Betty's fans around the world. Betty must have known that the end was near. Her condition worsened and, late at night at the Maynard on 7 February 1958, after periods in a coma, she died at the age of only fifty. Don and her daughters and all three of her sisters were at her bedside. The official cause of death was listed as 'Carcinomatosis', meaning there were multiple sites of cancer in her body.

Betty had requested no funeral service. Funerals were 'outmoded and barbaric rites', she once wrote. Her family asked that donations be sent to the American Cancer Society in lieu of flowers. She has no grave. She was cremated and her ashes probably sent to Don in California.

A few days later Blanche was at a symphony and met Mary in an elevator. The elevator was crowded but they made their way across to each other and hugged. No words were necessary.

Legacy

BETTY would have been the very last person in the world to put herself on a list of great writers. Her work might even be described as just enjoyably witty, an unusual mix of good descriptive writing and extreme sarcasm. She tends to be viewed as just one among a number of self-deprecating female humorists typical of the era. Arguably none of them, however, can match Betty's earthiness or acute wit, and none have married humor with her deeper insights into human joy and grief. The universality of her take on family life and on the pleasures and struggles of existence appeals to so many because she might be describing the life of each and every one of us, whatever our nationality: her books have enjoyed success all over the world. The sardonic amusement and hope for the future that Betty was able to find in even the hardest of times had particular resonance for Eastern European readers, for instance, who had suffered so many bitter times themselves. Her ability to take hardship and misfortune and transform them into something laughable certainly found an avid audience in Czechoslovakia. In 1988 a Czech fan wrote that Betty's books were beloved in her country because Betty looked at life with hope and faith that things would turn out for the best: her innate wisdom and sense of humor overcame all obstacles.

Betty also found enthusiastic fans in the UK. In 2008, the BBC broadcast a tribute program to commemorate the 100th anniversary of her birth, and the following year there was a BBC reading of *Anybody Can Do Anything*.

Bookselling websites still continue to reverberate with enthusiastic comments from fans in New Zealand, South Africa, Germany, Australia and elsewhere, and over the years there have been successive waves of demand for Betty's books to be reprinted. More than a few readers mention that their parents or grandparents loved the books and had introduced them to the next generation.

Betty's writing was a critical success at the time but there were later attacks on her negative portrayal of Native Americans, and the accusation that she 'spawned a perception of Washington as a land of eccentric country bumpkins like Ma and Pa Kettle'. Betty's defenders point out that in the context of the 1940s such stereotyping was ubiquitous and indeed acceptable. She was also concerned to represent Native Americans in a more realistic way than they had been depicted in many of the too reverential back-to-nature books which, in writing *Egg*, she was seeking to refute. It is true that modern readers will wince at her depiction of Native Americans as dirty, drunken and leering. These views also emerged a little in private correspondence (a letter whilst on her 1946 publicity tour referred to Native Americans making jewelry souvenirs to fit 'their big fat selves'). She even goes so far as to say in print that she is glad that the Native Americans' beautiful country has been taken away from them. It is difficult to read this now and hard to believe that Betty could ever have voiced such opinions, even if written in an era when such observations were commonplace. However, if episodes such as the invasion of the ranch during Bob's absence were rooted in reality, then it is at least understandable that Betty's fear may have translated into antipathy. In the Foreword to a much later edition of *The Egg and I* her daughters wrote that they were certain that if their mother were still alive she would address the plight of the Native American very differently, and that they knew she only meant to extract humor from what seemed to her to be frightening situations.

Similarly, Betty's attitude towards her Japanese fellow patient 'Kimi' in *The Plague and I* may sometimes smack of

Orientalism – she wrote that whatever 'Kimi' said always sounded as if it should be written on parchment with a spray of cherry blossoms – and she occasionally represented 'Kimi' as speaking with a heavy accent ('hahrible' for 'horrible'), even though her friend is well educated. But this, and some other racial stereotyping glimpsed in *Onions in the Stew*, are again aspects of common attitudes from the decades she was writing in. It was the 1940s and '50s and Betty was of her time and culture.

What is surely more telling is the way Betty steps beyond those boundaries. In *Anybody Can Do Anything*, Betty makes a point of observing sadly that the very capable young Japanese girls in her shorthand class will never be hired, no matter how proficient. Not just because of the Depression, she goes on, but because of the then common practice of seldom hiring any non-white office workers. Betty had no such prejudices. Whilst at the Firland sanatorium she became good friends with the young Japanese girl Monica Sone, the model for 'Kimi' in *Plague*, at a time when people routinely objected to sharing rooms with non-whites. Betty was more than happy to have Monica room with her, and in the book mentions how frequently she muses on her good fortune in having such an intelligent and considerate person as a fellow patient. When Betty is moved from a four-bed ward into a two-bed cubicle she delightedly agrees to have 'Kimi' moved in with her – she has grown to love her and wants her companionship. The nurse supervising the move is surprised and remarks that some people would object to sharing a room with an 'Oriental'. In real life Monica herself was also surprised, having expected only a white person to be chosen to share with Betty. The friendship continued after both had left the sanatorium.

Monica wanted to go to university and begged Betty to come to her home and help her convince her parents, which Betty gladly did, with success. Betty disagreed with the policy of Japanese internment and supported Monica and her family during their wartime incarceration, at a time when the Japanese in the US were held to be deeply suspect. She felt very sorry for those who could not find anywhere to stay after release from internment and, through the United States Relocation Center, offered her house on Vashon to a returning family for six months while she and Don were on a trip to New York.

After the war and her own publishing success Betty took Monica's extensive letters from the camps, which she had been keeping unbeknownst to her friend, to an editor at *The Atlantic Monthly Press*, who expressed interest. Betty told Monica that she should write a book about internment, expressing its horror but making it funny. If she herself could be funny about tuberculosis, she added, then Monica could be 'killing' about internment, now that it was over. This led to Monica's publication of her own successful memoir, *Nisei Daughter*, about growing up Japanese in America and about her family's internment during the war. Her publishers suggested that in her writing she should address a friendly, interested person as her reader, and of course Monica then pictured Betty. When the book came out Betty called round all the bookstores and newspapers in Seattle to drum up some reviews, and she provided her own endorsement on its back cover - the only book ever to have one, despite numerous requests:

The internment of the American-born Japanese during the last war is handled with honesty and rare dispassion. It is certainly to Monica Sone's credit that she still sings 'God Bless America.'

There is further evidence to counter those who cry racism. In *The Plague and I* Betty described sharing a bathroom at the sanatorium with an African American woman she called Evalee. It's indicative that Betty sympathetically includes Evalee's remarks on the difficulties she encounters in the institute as a non-white. Her bed has been put outside on a porch because it solves the 'room-mate problem'. White patients would object to sharing a room with her, Evalee tells Betty, and even on the porch, where the beds are quite far apart, there are complaints. Using a racial epithet, another patient remarks to Betty that Evalee won't last long because her race has no resistance to tuberculosis. Betty sharply tells the patient not to call Evalee by that word. Later, Evalee is a welcome member of Betty's close band of friends in the Ambulant Hospital who gather together in the bedrooms to drink tea and commiserate with each other about their woes.

Betty's pluses and minuses on this particular scoresheet must be judged by posterity. Meanwhile, she merits more of a niche than she currently holds in the pantheon of 20th-century American women writers, most particularly for her regionalism – her acute talent for capturing local color in the Pacific Northwest. *Seattle Times* book critic Michael Upchurch declared that had Betty been born in New York her reputation would have been as assured as Dorothy Parker's, while the award-winning writer Jonathan Raban placed Betty on his list of essential reading about his adopted city of Seattle (observing also that his grandmother used to have a copy of *The Egg and I* on her bookshelf in England).

But Betty has never been ranked with classic regional writers such as Harper Lee or Willa Cather, perhaps because her works are humorous 'memoirs' rather than serious novels. Nevertheless, Professor Beth Kraig in her 2005 study, *It's About Time Somebody Out Here Wrote The Truth: Betty Bard MacDonald and North/Western Regionalism*, argues that Betty is indeed a regionalist, but not in the classic mold; rather, she is a modern, mid-20th-century regional writer anxious to paint a true picture of her beloved country but at the same time to dispel over-romantic perceptions. Mary points out to Betty in *Anybody* that the world needs to know the real Northwest, to understand that salmon no longer leap in at the front door and snap at their ankles. In a timely reversal of mythic notions of heroic pioneering, Betty duly reveals a country with big cities as well as wide-open spaces, a land scarred from mining and logging and sometimes strained by racial tensions; a Northwest of dock towns, ferry strikes, mountains, and rain-washed city lights. And a part of her message, Professor Kraig's study posits, is that beautiful scenery and magnificent mountains cannot always compensate for hardship and loneliness.

Other academic works have viewed *The Egg and I* through the prism of gender politics. Professor Nancy Walker, for example, lumps Betty with the 'domestic humorists' of postwar American suburbia such as Jean Kerr (*Please Don't Eat the Daisies*) or Phyllis McGinley, who shared with Betty the use of self-deprecation as a major source of their humor and as a subversive device. Professor Walker suggests that underlying the cheerful surface of this sort of writing is a sense of uneasiness with the isolation of the housewife and with male remoteness and domination, and that confessions of inability and inefficiency in the role of housewife are a subtle way of subverting societal norms. A classic pattern is presented of a husband who enjoys the challenges of his work while the wife is left to cope with the routine tasks of household and children; the contrast between the two points up the staggering difference between gender roles and the wife's resultant discontent.

Another insightful analysis of *The Egg and I* by Jane F. Levey likewise considers the work primarily an expression of postwar dissatisfaction with the role of housewife and mother. This study argues that books often become popular because they address a pressing cultural issue or anxiety; according to Levey, *Egg* was primarily an account of Betty's resistance to her wifely role and, as such, spoke to specific contemporary concerns in the 1940s. As their husbands in the military returned from the war and needed their jobs back, women who had been in the armed forces or who had worked in factories and offices were encouraged to return to the home, and many were unhappy with this reappearance of traditional gender divisions. Levey attributes the book's phenomenal success, which came as a huge surprise to the publishing industry, to this capturing of the gender zeitgeist. Although the book was set in the past, she argues that *Egg* voiced women's postwar concerns. She, too, sees Betty's acid observations on a wife's 'bounden duty to see that her husband is happy in his work' as sharply probing the husband-wife relationship, and as a questioning of women's assignment to household duties and the isolation of domesticity. Levey points out that Betty reserved her greatest affection for the slovenly Ma Kettle, while expressing disdain and pity for the model housewife character Mrs Hicks. Other critiques of housework and the confines of motherhood appearing at the time did not of course attain *Egg*'s popularity because they lacked its humorous delivery, which in Jane Levey's view deflected many from what she saw as its serious feminist message.

The feminist argument may not stand up to scrutiny. Once married to Don MacDonald, Betty happily made a home and declared that she was first, last and always a wife and mother. (She even, of her own volition, returned to canning.) As a writer she is left in limbo: not viewed as among the classic regionalists, and arguably not truly in the vanguard of feminism, while her anecdotal style, the affectionate focus on her rambunctious family, and what the *New York Times* critic Bosley Crowther termed the 'earthy tang' of her writing may not suggest a serious author. But taken together, her gift for local color, her wifely skepticism, and the anecdotes and intimate details of work and home life all combine to provide an accurate picture of significant times in America: homesteading, Depression, war, and finally the growing prosperity of the mid-20th century. Betty MacDonald's lightly fictionalized accounts of her life in the Northwest in the 1920s-1950s, shot through with an acerbic commentary on the people and manners she saw around her, are authentic gems encapsulating a place and a time in history.

There are no monuments to Betty, no endowments or scholarships, only the renamed stretch of two-lane road passing the chicken farm where she lived for four long years: Egg and I Road.

Afterword

BETTY'S will was admitted to probate on 5 May 1958 in Seattle. Press reported that Betty left her share of the Vashon home to Don; seemingly, it had still not been sold. Most of the remainder of her estate, valued at more than $60,000, was in California and was to be probated separately in Monterey. Her 'community' half (probably meaning everything that Betty and Don owned together), other than the Vashon property, was bequeathed to Anne and Joan.

To recoup the loss on their advance for Betty's fifth *Mrs. Piggle-Wiggle* book, which never transpired, Lippincott took extracts from her four works and produced *Who, Me?*, marketing it as Betty's autobiography. No new material was included. Lippincott and Betty's agent Bernice did consider weaving in quotes from some of Betty's letters to them both. The idea was abandoned. Betty often let rip in these missives and the tone could be too caustic, especially about individuals, and there was reluctance to reveal this aspect of Betty in print. The Lippincott editor who worked on *Who, Me?* remarked that Betty's character had comprised a collection of contradictory qualities and that Betty was a particularly complex person.

According to Betty's sister Mary in 1959, there was considerable unpublished material among Betty's belongings, including an entire novel (likely to be the early novel version of *Onions*) and an uncompleted collection of stories for the *Mrs Piggle-Wiggle* series. Rumors of the novel surfaced again in 1982 when Betty's daughter Joan mentioned in an interview that a publisher's representative had the manuscript of an unpublished novel which had been found among Betty's papers. Joan also had her mother's letters, which she described as 'hysterically funny', meant only for Betty's mother and sisters and not for public consumption. All the Bards set great store by funny letter-writing. If you wrote a dull letter, Betty once told an interviewer, you were asked if you had lost your wits, and next time you worked harder to make it amusing. Not by faking, but by giving the details that made a situation funny or interesting. 'In this family you've got to talk and write fairly sharply or admit you're a dope.'

People

Betty's husband Donald MacDonald stayed on at the ranch after Betty's death and continued to raise cattle, selling off pieces of the property when he needed money. There was little contact with Anne or Joan or the rest of the family, although both encouraged their offspring to write and thank Don for presents. Many readers were unaware that Betty had died and for decades fan letters continued to be forwarded to Don from Lippincott; he stored them, unopened, with her other papers. He often neglected to attend to correspondence or business matters and would fail to sign documents relating to the later licensing of Betty's work, much to the rest of the family's frustration.

In 1975, when he was sixty-five, Don caught the flu and was in bed alone for several weeks. Finally feeling better, he got up and dressed but fell down the front steps as he was going out. When the ranch manager reached him,

Don was unconscious. An ambulance was called and he was taken to the local hospital, but he had suffered a heart attack and never regained consciousness. Machines kept his breathing going but Don was brain dead and the machinery was disconnected after about a week.

Betty's first daughter Anne MacDonald had four children and was married three times, to Donald Strunk, Robert Evans and Donald Ray Canham. After Don MacDonald died in 1975 Anne and her son Darsie Evans moved onto the ranch but, after several years of dispute with Joan about the property, it was eventually sold.

In 2001 Anne told a Carmel Valley newsletter that she was finally writing her first book after having promised her mother over forty years ago that she would be a writer. She was already a successful artist and said that the inspiration for her oil painting came from her wonderful, talented grandmother Sydney Bard, who had patiently taught her so much when she was a child. Anne exhibited her works throughout the US, Canada and Japan. In 2007 she published *Happy Birthday, Mrs. Piggle-Wiggle*, based on stories and characters created by Betty. The book is attributed to both mother and daughter.

Betty's second daughter Joan MacDonald and husband Jerry Keil had four children and lived near Seattle. Long after Betty died, Joan, along with Anne, was still receiving so many fan letters from children, mothers, grandmothers, teachers and librarians wanting *Nancy and Plum* to be reprinted that she decided to lobby publishers for a new edition. Joan was unable to secure a deal so in 1982 she and a friend formed the Betty MacDonald Memorial Publishing Company, planning to republish all her mother's books. Joan had intended to call her enterprise the Anybody Can Do Anything Company, but instead they selected the ultimate name as a 'tribute and resurrection of Betty MacDonald'. The first of their efforts was *Nancy and Plum*, which appeared in Seattle stores that year in time for Christmas. Joan announced that 5% of all present and future sales of the book would be donated to the Children's Orthopedic Hospital 'in the name of Betty MacDonald for all the children everywhere'. The book went out of print again but the letters kept coming, so in 1997 Joan republished *Nancy and Plum* for the second time, having formed the Joan Keil Enterprises company somewhere along the way. Joan often gave talks about Betty at libraries and schools and like her mother was very creative: she loved to paint, garden, cook and arrange flowers, and she also sang in variety shows to help raise money for charity. And, just like Betty, Joan's sense of humor always made people laugh. She died in 2004 at the age of 75, in Bellevue, Washington.

Betty's sister Mary Bard was left bereft by the loss of her sister. Reflecting on their relationship shortly after Betty's death, she told Bernice Baumgarten that Betty had furnished their imaginative lives, and that she had provided the practical. In her opinion the two of them combined had become Sydney's husband and managed her children. Their common fault, in Mary's eyes, was that they needed the praise and faith that each provided for the other. Apart from that, they were not in the least alike, Mary declared. They loved and admired each other but disagreed on almost everything.

Mary wrote several books herself, including successful children's books and her best-known work *The Doctor Wears Three Faces* (dedicated to Betty, who 'egged me on'). In 1950 the book was turned into a movie entitled *Mother Didn't Tell Me,* starring Dorothy McGuire, June Havoc, and Leif Erickson. Like Betty, Mary promoted her work around the country and on national radio and became a Seattle celebrity, although her books never sold in the millions as Betty's had. A projected book about Sydney fell apart when Mary told Lippincott that she just didn't know their mother well enough.

She remained an active participant in Seattle community life and in the late 1960s volunteered to teach play writing in schools in Seattle's Central Area, despite the racial unrest there at the time. One of the leaders of the Seattle chapter of the Black Panthers used to provide a safe passage for Mary through the volatile location, meeting her each week downtown and driving her to her volunteer work himself. Mary suffered a stroke and died on Vashon in 1970 at the age of sixty-six.

Betty's brother Cleve Bard graduated from Roosevelt High and was married twice, first to Margaret Tracy in 1933. He had two sons with his second wife Mary Alice. He is buried in Vashon Island Cemetery.

Betty's sister Dede (Dorothea Darsie) Bard graduated from Roosevelt High and embarked on a singing career. She married Melvin Goldsmith in 1943, and had three sons. She died in 1994.

Betty's youngest sister Alison Bard graduated from Roosevelt High and first married Frank Sugia, a well-known jazz accordionist and bandleader on the Northwest music scene. With their infant son Darsie they moved to Vashon one year after Betty, in 1943, but then divorced following the birth of their second son Bard in 1945. Alison married Bernard Beck in 1946 and their daughter was born in 1948. The family moved to Mercer Island in the 1950s and there Alison began a long career in real-estate sales. In the mid 1960s she divorced and in the early 1970s married William Burnett. They lived in

Kailua-Kona, Hawaii, Scottsdale, Arizona and Kirkland, Washington, where William Burnett died in 1978. Alison loved to entertain, was a passionate gardener, wonderful cook, talented decorator, and a gifted writer. She loved music, especially jazz, and was an amazing dancer. She loved dogs and was a fierce champion of fairness. Alison died in 2009 at the age of eighty-nine.

Alison's son Darsie Beck became a well-known artist on Vashon. When he was a little boy Betty and the girls often took care of him while Alison worked, and he remembered countless adventures on the beach and parties at the house, and a kitchen that was always the hub of all the fun. Darsie recalled those years with Betty and her daughters as very creative; art was just part of the entertainment. He is the author of *Your Essential Nature, A Practical Guide to Greater Creativity and Spiritual Harmony*, a workbook describing his long practice of daily writing, drawing and meditation.

Betty's dear friend Blanche Caffiere died in 2006 at the age of 100, after a long career as teacher, author and librarian. One of Blanche's students was Microsoft founder Bill Gates, who worked as her school library assistant. He later credited his philanthropic efforts to introduce computer technology into school libraries to Blanche's early encouragement of his own studies and her insistence on the importance of reading. Her 1992 book about her life and friendship with Betty and the Bards, *Much Laughter, A Few Tears*, has provided fans and scholars with valuable insights into Betty's life and work. The book was also published in Czechoslovakia where Betty MacDonald was still extremely popular. The interest there in Blanche's memoir took the 94-year-old Blanche to Prague where she was feted, interviewed on television, and mobbed by autograph seekers. She was a popular public speaker in the US also and appeared as part of the Vashon Island Library's anniversary celebrations in October 2006, when she stood for nearly an hour sharing memories of Vashon and her dear friend Betty.

Monica Sone ('Kimi' in *The Plague and I*) grew up in Seattle, where her parents, immigrants from Japan, managed a hotel. During World War II she and her family were interned at Puyallup Civilian Assembly Center and at the Minidoka War Relocation Center in Hunt, Idaho. In 1942, Monica was allowed to leave the camp to attend college in Indiana, where she lived with a local family. She eventually gained a master's degree in clinical psychology. Her best-known work is the 1953 memoir *Nisei Daughter*, which tells the story of Japanese immigrant family life in the United States before and during the war, and in which she writes of her friendship with Betty ('Chris') at Firland sanatorium. Monica passed away in 2011 at the age of 92.

Places

In 1967, when the *Egg and I* farm was for sale, it had a new, three-bed house and two-car garage but some of the same stately cedars and other timber still stood on the forty acres as they had done in Betty's day. The house offered a 'tremendous view of Olympics', a good well and hunting on the property. The school bus stopped at the door.

The shingled house at 6317 15th Avenue in Seattle, where Betty and her family lived in the 1930s, no longer exists. The house had many occupants after Betty and her family moved away, and then slowly deteriorated. On 24 July 2012 the house was demolished.

The house on Vashon Island where Betty wrote her books is now a private residence but the surrounding woods and orchards remain unchanged. Two of the subsequent owners have also been writers. The huge barn that the MacDonalds built on their land, painted red with white trim, is operating as a Bed and Breakfast.

The Bishop farm in Chimacum on the Olympic Peninsula remains in the family and is now run as an organic dairy farm.

Bibliography and References

Ament, Deloris Tarzan, historylink.org, Essay 5221 (about William Cumming)

American Women's Club of Amsterdam, *OPIJNEN – The Dutch Village That Still Cares*, Tulip Talk newsletter May 1983

Anne and Joan MacDonald, A Common Reader interview, 1998; Foreword to 1987 Harper and Row Perennial edition of *The Egg and I*

Arts News (Vashon Allied Arts), *Vashon Island was home to Betty MacDonald*, March 1988

Bard, Mary, *Forty Odd*, J. B. Lippincott, 1952

Bard, Mary, *The Doctor Wears Three Faces*, J. B. Lippincott, 1949

Baumgarten, Bernice, letters to Betty MacDonald, Baumgarten mss., Lilly Library, Indiana University

Beck, Darsie, *E S Bard Drawings and Paintings*

Becker, Paula, historylink.org, Essays 3928, 7035, 8261, 8263, 8267, 8270, 8271, 8273, 10155, 10346, 10715

Bellingham Herald

Bishop, Edward Leroy, oral history, Jefferson County Historical Society, Port Townsend, Washington

Boulder Daily Camera

Burnett, Alison Bard, Epilog to Blanche Caffiere's *Much Laughter, A Few Tears*

Caffiere, Blanche, *Much Laughter, A Few Tears*, Blue Gables Publishing, 1992

Callahan, Margaret Bundy, *Story of a Full Life*, Seattle Times, 3 July 1949 (about Sydney Bard)

Callahan, Margaret Bundy, Papers, University of Washington Special Collections

Carmel Valley Newsletter, *The Art of Anne Canham*, January 2001

Chinn, Ray historylink.org Essay 9333 (University District oral history)

Cumming, William, *Sketchbook: A Memoir of the 1930s and the Northwest School*, Seattle: University of Washington Press, 1984

Daily Chronicle (Centralia, Washington)

Daily Olympian

Dederer, Claire, *Her Great Depression*, Columbia Journalism Review, January/February 2011

Dorpat, Paul historylink.org Essay 3380 (about the University District)

Gravelle, Randal *Hooverville and the Unemployed: Seattle during the Great Depression*

Gregory, James, *Economics and Poverty* The Great Depression in Washington State Project, https://depts.washington.edu/depress/economics_poverty.shtml (retrieved 2015)

Hamley, Frederick G. *Firland: A Story of Firland Sanatorium*, Seattle: Firland Occupational Therapy Department, ca. 1937

Hart, James D., *The Popular Book*, University of California Press, 1950

Hoekstra, Samantha, *The Egg and Us: Contextualization and Historicization of Betty MacDonald's Works*, thesis, Florida State University, 2014

https://www.youtube.com/watch?v=LTaZaqAIjagMe Betty in movie trailer

https://www.youtube.com/watch?v=IvaZivR6UcE Betty in newsreel

Jefferson County records

Jensen, Mary Bard, letters

Kindig, Jessie, *Culture and Arts during the Depression*, The Great Depression in Washington State Project, https://depts.washington.edu/depress/culture_arts.shtml (retrieved 2015)

King County records

Kraig, Beth, *Betty and the Bishops: Was The Egg and I Libelous?* Columbia Magazine, Spring 1998: Vol. 12, No. 1.

Kraig, Beth, *It's About Time Somebody Out Here Wrote the Truth: Betty Bard MacDonald and North/West Regionalism* Western American Literature 40.3 (Fall 2005): 237-71

Laughlin, Helen MacDonald, sister of Donald MacDonald (description of death of Donald MacDonald)

Levey, Jane F., *Imagining the Family in U.S. Popular Postwar Culture: The Case of The Egg and I and Cheaper by the Dozen*, Journal of Women's History, 13.3 (Autumn 2001), Johns Hopkins University Press

Life magazine, *Life Goes Calling on the Author of The Egg and I,* March 18 1946

MacDonald, Betty, letters, 15 July 1945 (to Mrs. Forrest, Folder V.F. 844 Betty Bard MacDonald Papers, University of Washington); 14 Feb 1946 (to Mary Bard Jensen); 5 Sept 1947 (to Hazel); 6 February 1954 (to Bertram Lippincott); 26 Jan 1956 (to Blanche Caffiere); 2 July 1956 (to Blanche Caffiere); to Bernice Baumgarten (1944 - 1957)

MacDonald, Betty, radio interview with George Fisher, USC Cinematic Arts Library Universal-International Pictures Collection

MacDonald, Betty, *Anybody Can Do Anything,* Philadelphia: J. B. Lippincott, 1950

MacDonald, Betty, *I'm an Optimist!* Farm Journal, January 1956

MacDonald, Betty, *Money and I,* Cosmopolitan, June 1949

MacDonald, Betty, *Onions in the Stew,* Philadelphia: J. B. Lippincott, 1955

MacDonald, Betty, *The Egg and I,* Philadelphia: J. B. Lippincott, 1945

MacDonald, Betty, *The Most Unforgettable Character I've Met,* Reader's Digest, July 1949; *An Unforgettable Character,* Reader's Digest, February 1954

MacDonald, Betty, *The Plague and I,* Philadelphia: J. B. Lippincott, 1948

MacDonald, Betty, *Their Families*, Town Crier magazine, 1933. Discovered by Paula Becker in the archives of the Seattle Public Library.

News Record (Vashon), 13 Feb 1958 (death of Betty MacDonald)

Newsweek, May 16, 1955 (review of *Onions in the Stew*)

New York Times, 1946, 1948

Oregonian, March 1903 (Sydney's wedding)

Oxnard Press Courier, 24 July 1955 (death of Robert Heskett)

Port Townsend Leader

Roosevelt High, Alumni records

Royer, Bob *Our Norwegian Boys Move on After the 1926 Rose Bowl* (about George Guttormsen) http://www.thecascadiacourier.com/search/label/Cascadia

S'Klallam tribal history, https://www.pgst.nsn.us/land-and-people-and-lifestyle/history

Seattle Post-Intelligencer

Seattle Daily and Sunday Times, 1919-1982

Seattle Times, 16 Sept 1951, 26 Nov 2006 (Blanche Caffiere obituary)

Seattle Weekly, 4 March 2008 http://www.seattleweekly.com/2008-03-05/news/how-puget-sound-s-last-pirate-gave-us-a-creaking-sinking-ferry-system/

Sone, Monica, *Nisei Daughter*, University of Washington Press, 1979

Starbuck, Susan, *Hazel Wolf: Fighting the Establishment*, Seattle: University of Washington Press, 2002, 112-116. historylink.org Essay 8801

Stars and Stripes, July 1951 (death of Robert Heskett)

State of Washington King County Clerk's Office, *Elizabeth B. Heskett v. Robert E. Heskett* Final Decree of Divorce, 8 March, 1935

State of Washington King County Superior Court, records

Stivers, George L., MD, *Closing of Tuberculous Lung Cavities by Intrapleural Pneumolysis*, N Engl J Med 1933; 208:469-479 March 2, 1933 DOI: 10.1056/NEJM193303022080901, New England Journal of Medicine

Strenuous Life For 1924, The Roosevelt High School yearbook

Stubbs, Frederick D., *Closed Intrapleural Pneumolysis in the Treatment of Pulmonary Tuberculosis (A Preliminary Report of Forty Operations)*, J Natl Med Assoc. May 1939

Sunday Herald-Boston, 22 March 1903 (Sydney's wedding)

Sunday Oregonian

Tate, Cassandra, historylink.org Essay 598 (about Burton and Florence James)

University of Washington, records

U.S. Federal Census, records

Universal-International Pictures Collection, University of Southern California, Los Angeles

Van Gelder, Robert, *Interview with a Best-Selling Author: Betty MacDonald*, Cosmopolitan November 1947

vashonhistory.com

Vashon-Maury Island Beachcomber, Joan MacDonald Keil obituary, 28 July 2004

Vashon-Maury Island Beachcomber, *MacDonald's centennial reminds Vashon of her place on the Island*, 26 April 2008

Vashon Heritage Museum Archive, Betty MacDonald Collection, Vashon Island

Vogel, Michelle, *Marjorie Main: The Life and Films of Hollywood's 'Ma Kettle'*, McFarland & Co Inc, 15 Jun 2011

Walker, Nancy, *Humor and Gender Roles: The 'Funny' Feminism of the Post-War World II Suburbs*, American Quarterly, Spring 1985, Volume XXXVII, Number 1

Washington State Archives, Puget Sound Regional Office, records

Wilkins, William J., *The Sword and the Gavel: An Autobiography by the Last of the Nuremberg Judges*, The Writing Works, Seattle, 1981

Wise, Ronald R, Bishop family memoir, http://leonidus.home.mindspring.com/bishops.htm

Printed in Great Britain
by Amazon